~ Love's ~
UNSEEN
ENEMY

How to Overcome Guilt to Build Healthy Relationships

DR. LES PARROTT III

HarperPaperbacks
New York, New York

ZondervanPublishingHouse
Grand Rapids, Michigan

Divisions of HarperCollinsPublishers

All scripture quotations, unless otherwise indicated, are taken
from the *Holy Bible: New International Edition*®. *NIV*®.
Copyright © 1973, 1978, 1984 by International Bible Society.
Used by permission of ZondervanPublishingHouse.

If you purchased this book without a cover, you should be aware
that this book is stolen property. It was reported as "unsold and
destroyed" to the publisher and neither the author nor the
publisher has received any payment for this "stripped book."

HarperPaperbacks   *A Division of* HarperCollins*Publishers*
10 East 53rd Street, New York, N.Y. 10022

Copyright © 1994 by Les Parrott III
All rights reserved. No part of this book may be used or repro-
duced in any manner whatsoever without written permission of
the publisher, except in the case of brief quotations embodied in
critical articles and reviews. For information address
ZondervanPublishingHouse, Grand Rapids, Michigan 49530.

A hardcover edition of this book was published in 1994
by ZondervanPublishingHouse, a division of
HarperCollins*Publishers*.

First HarperPaperbacks printing: June 1996

Printed in the United States of America

HarperPaperbacks and colophon are trademarks of
HarperCollins*Publishers*

❖ 10 9 8 7 6 5 4 3 2 1

002500

"Dr. Parrott helps us understand and remedy guilt's impact on our personal relationships. Read these pages. You will be the better for it."

—Dr. Archibald D. Hart
Dean and Professor of Psychology
Fuller Theological Seminary

"How many times have I been on a guilt trip needing an exit! This book offers a proven route to recovery so we as Christians can live a guilt-free life."

—Barbara Johnson
Author of *Stick a Geranium in Your Hat and Be Happy*

"Dr. Parrott has done a wonderful job of giving us a sensitive, insightful, biblical understanding of guilt's binding chains and the path to freedom."

—Dr. Bruce Narramore
Distinguished Professor of Psychology
Biola University

"Les has nailed the primary 'hidden' cause of the destruction of relationships. This book gets 'two thumbs up' from me."

—Stephen Arterburn
Founder, New Life Treatment Center

"A hope-giving message for all of us. Les Parrott has hit a critical topic."

—Dr. Grace
Author of *Mothering*

ATTENTION: ORGANIZATIONS AND CORPORATIONS

Most HarperPaperbacks are available at special quantity discounts for bulk purchases for sales promotions, premiums, or fund-raising. For information, please call or write:
**Special Markets Department, HarperCollins*Publishers*,
10 East 53rd Street, New York, N.Y. 10022.**
Telephone: (212) 207-7528. Fax: (212) 207-7222.

To Leslie,
my wife and best friend

CONTENTS

ACKNOWLEDGMENTS

When Leslie and I gathered with the Zondervan people at their corporate headquarters in Grand Rapids, it was like coming home. Their support and enthusiasm for this project reassured and motivated me. They are thoroughly professional people but also delightfully human. I owe special gratitude to Scott Bolinder, Vice President and Publisher, whose vision of our working relationship began like an epiphany at dinner one evening in Atlanta.

When I asked my editor, Sandy Vander Zicht, and her associate, Lori Walburg, to teach me the art of writing well, I had no idea how much would be required on their part and on mine. Their standards are pervasive and persistent. Their tough-minded readings of the manuscript elevated its style and substance. Best of all, they never made me feel guilty over the inevitable pushing back of our deadlines.

I am also grateful to Christine Anderson, advertising manager at Zondervan. She believed in me and in this project since our first discussions in Berkeley, California. Thanks, Christine.

The seeds of this book were planted in a research project that flowered into more than a decade of personal study and writing. Dr. Bruce Narramore was especially influential in shaping my thinking. His book *No Condemnation* was the catalyst for my studies. I owe him a great debt.

I have been fortunate to tap into the insights and guidance of many teachers, colleagues, and friends who have made this journey a learning pilgrimage. They include Dr. Archibald Hart, Dr. Newton Malony, Dr. Ronald Benefiel, Dr. Stephen Moore, the Rev. Tharon Daniels, Dr. Dennis Guernsey, Dr. Joy Hammersla, Dr. Míchael Row, and Dr.

Delbert McHenry. Thank you, one and all, for what you have contributed to me and to this project. And thank you for keeping my feet to the fire.

John Woodyard, Drew Anderson, and all of the board who worked with us at the Murdock Charitable Trust deserve special appreciation for helping Leslie and me establish the Center for Relationship Development at Seattle Pacific University. This book will serve as a tool in the Center's mission to foster healthy relationships.

I appreciate my colleagues at Seattle Pacific University, who understand and encourage my calling to integrate spiritual values with human understanding. I must also acknowledge my appreciation and respect for a host of students, clients, and patients, who entrusted me with inside knowledge of their private and painful journeys. They have taught me much.

I have always known that writing was a serious part of my calling. But it was not until writing this book that I realized how much the craft of writing is a part of my makeup. It has become obvious to me that I have inherited a love for the majesty of the declarative sentence and the cadence of words rightly used. The blood of two authors courses through my veins. Thanks, Mom and Dad. Your optimism and affection are a source of inspiration too easily taken for granted.

The dedication of this book is not made lightly. My wife, Leslie, has walked extra miles with me again and again during this project. She has endured endless discussions about love and guilt and has listened to me talk about it in hundreds of lectures, seminars, and sermons. She has interacted with the material while on vacation, over dinner, and after the lights are turned out. It is difficult for me to imagine how any human being could give more to another than Leslie has given to me. Because of her patience, understanding, and unswerving dedication, our relationship knows no bounds. Nor does my love for her.

Les Parrott III
Seattle, Washington

INTRODUCTION

For five hours I stood beside a neurosurgeon in a sterile operating room and watched him patiently and skillfully remove a malignant growth from an otherwise healthy spinal cord.

Later, as I drove out of the hospital parking lot, the thought hit me that I, as a psychologist, needed to perform my own delicate surgery. My patient, Linda, a married woman in her late thirties, was unaware of a cancerous emotion that was quietly eating away at her most cherished relationships. We couldn't x-ray the problem. But if we could have, the films would have revealed a common unseen enemy — feelings of guilt and shame.

After a decade of research, involving thousands of people, I have seen guilt emerge again and again as love's unseen enemy. I have carefully studied guilt's prevalence, frequency, and significance. And I have found, to my alarm, that a dangerous undercurrent of guilt flows through every unhealthy relationship.

Take Linda, for example. My client lived to please. She yearned for acceptance and approval. She was always willing to lend a hand, even at great inconvenience. The more sweat and self-sacrifice the favor required, the more eager Linda was to help. She ran a nonstop race to convince herself and everyone else that she was truly loving.

Linda's life was governed by a single misguided belief: To be a loving person, I must win the approval of others. Because she subscribed to this notion, she focused her attention on performance rather than personhood. Her energy was spent on *doing* loving things rather than *being* a loving person.

Whenever Linda couldn't comply with someone's

request, she felt guilty. And because she felt guilty, she had no room to feel joy, love, or intimacy. In fact, her deeds of love had degenerated into unfulfilling duties. Linda desperately wanted to love and be loved, but the more she chased after love, the more elusive it became.

The afternoon I drove away from the hospital, I longed for a psychological scalpel to cut away Linda's malignant guilt. Unfortunately, an operation to remove a guilt-prone conscience does not exist. I had only the painstaking remedy of counseling. In the counseling process, Linda and I worked together to combat guilt, her unseen enemy. Only when she squarely faced guilt and exposed its secret destruction of love could she begin to build healthy relationships.

Maybe you, too, are longing for authentic, intimate relationships. Maybe you, too, are stalked by love's unseen enemy—guilt. This book will unmask that enemy, revealing the guilt-prone conscience. And it will give you the weapons you need to fight guilt, as well as the tools you need to build healthy relationships.

Perhaps you are unaware of how the emotion of guilt has seeped into your psyche and sabotaged your relationships. Or perhaps you are on the receiving end of guilt-motivated love and are yearning for something more. In either case, this book will help you cut the malignancy of irrational guilt out of your relationships before it becomes terminal.

Part One

Part One

EXPOSING THE UNSEEN
ENEMY

1

Identifying the Unseen Enemy: A Self-Test

I have a friend, Allen, who works at home. One morning Allen discovered that his computer drive would not accept a disk. Tyler, his three-year-old son, watched as Allen tried repeatedly, without success, to get the computer to accept the disk.

"Maybe there's a penny in the hole," Tyler suggested.

Sure enough, Allen spied a penny in the narrow slot and eventually extracted it with tweezers. But the drive still would not take the disk. Watching Allen grumble in frustration, Tyler suggested, "Maybe there's *lots* of pennies in there."

Tyler identified the problem, and his father then found the solution. As this story illustrates, identifying the problem is often the key to finding its solution. Time and time again, for example, counselors have to make their clients *aware* of their problems. Once a client sees his problem clearly, he can often then take the necessary steps to solve his problem.

In this book, we will focus on the problem of guilt. We will look at how guilt interferes with our relationships and how it prevents us from functioning correctly. Once we can identify guilt and recognize its destructive effects on our lives, we can then take steps to reduce its hold on us.

WATCH FOR THE CAMOUFLAGE

Guilt often goes unnoticed. Nobody comes into my office complaining that guilt is ruining his relationships. In fact, few people suspect it is the culprit in their relational problems. Let me illustrate what I mean.

A factory was having problems with employee theft. Every day someone stole a valuable item. So the plant hired a security guard to search each employee as he or she left the building. Most employees carried only a lunch pail. But every day at closing time one man took a wheelbarrow full of trash, which the exasperated security guard had to dig through to determine whether he was making off with anything of value.

The guard never found anything in the trash, but one day he could stand it no longer. "Look," he said, "I know you're up to something, but I can never find anything worth stealing in all that trash you carry out. It's driving me crazy. Just tell me what you're up to, and I promise not to report you."

The man shrugged and said, "Wheelbarrows. I'm taking wheelbarrows."

The guilt infecting relationships is like the brazen camouflage of the wheelbarrows. Guilt does not try to hide, but it diverts attention from itself. Like the security guard in this story, people can work so hard at finding reasons for their relational difficulties that they miss the real problem of guilt. They feel its work in their consciences, but seldom suspect it as the root cause of their problems.

Guilt may drive the employee who sets up a no-win situation with his boss. Guilt may be the reason a woman squirms uncomfortably when a compliment comes her way, because she feels she doesn't deserve praise. Guilt can even be converted into physical symptoms, hiding incognito in an illness, in an unconscious attempt at self-punishment.

Guilt does its deeds in countless ways, some more obvious than others. But it often works in camouflage, deep in the corners of our lives. In this chapter we will try to pick up guilt's scent, track it down, and smoke it out.

TESTING YOUR LEVEL OF GUILT

The following questionnaire will help you measure your level of guilt. There are no right or wrong answers. Take as much time as you need. Answer each item as carefully and as accurately as you can by placing a number beside each of the items as follows:

1 Rarely or none of the time
2 A little of the time
3 Some of the time
4 A good part of the time
5 Most or all of the time

_____ I worry about what others think of me.

_____ I believe I should always be generous.

_____ I feel I should be punished.

_____ I believe I am guilty.

_____ I believe I should not be angry.

_____ I take a hard look at myself.

_____ I feel ashamed.

_____ I punish myself.

_____ I detest myself for my failures.

_____ A guilty conscience bothers me.

_____ I believe I should not lose my temper.

_____ I feel guilty.

_____ I am fretful.

_____ When I feel guilty, it lasts a long time.

_____ I feel I am unforgivable.

_____ I feel I am a reject.

_____ I detest myself for my thoughts.

_____ I feel nervous about others' opinions of me.

_____ I believe I should not hurt another person's feelings.

_____ I fear something bad will happen to me in the future.

_____ I have spells of very intense guilt.

_____ I avoid some places due to my guilt feelings.

_____ I cannot tell the difference between feeling guilty and being guilty.

_____ I avoid some people due to my guilt feelings.

_____ I avoid being alone because of my guilt feelings.

Score this self-test by totaling up your points on the items and subtracting 25. This gives a potential score of 0 to 100. Although this test is not a failproof diagnostic tool, it will help you measure the intensity of your guilt feelings.

Total   _____

    _____
    -25
    _____

Score   _____

80–100 You are wracked with feelings of guilt. You are in serious need of professional help and should seek psychotherapy as soon as possible.

60–79 You may not be in immediate need of professional help, but you aren't out of the danger zone. You could benefit from the assistance of a professional counselor, who can help you process your struggle with guilt.

40–59 You are in the guilt trap, and guilt has probably taken its toll on your relationships. However, you are in a good position for using practical tools that can help you escape.

20–39 You are on your way to escaping the guilt trap. Your experiences with a nagging conscience are temporary, and you are not allowing your guilt to get the best of you. While you do not need an overhaul, you can benefit from some fine tuning.

0–19 You are certainly free from irrational guilt and have what it takes to lay a solid foundation for healthy relationships. You will want to be aware of how you can help others who struggle with guilt. However, if your score is extremely low, you may have an undeveloped conscience that will lead to other difficulties.

I am not so naive as to believe guilt can be pinpointed and tagged with a number. But a self-test can help us catch a glimpse of this illusive emotion. To examine more accurately the personal intricacies of guilt requires deep, earnest soul-searching. And the expedition sometimes involves excavating emotional artifacts that have long been buried.

WHAT MAKES PEOPLE FEEL GUILTY?

Guilt is universal, striking people of all ages everywhere. I have listened to guilt stories from all kinds of people: working mothers, top-notch students, homeless victims, sincere pastors, war veterans, competent counselors, engaged couples, divorced parents, and successful business executives. No one is exempt. Sooner or later, in some place, at some time, the feelings of guilt arise, disrupting relationships and leaving its victims in pain.

"Guilt feels deep and almost physical," one of my patients said. And she's not alone. In a survey of one thousand women of varying backgrounds from across the nation, guilt was found to be their greatest emotional problem. Some experts call guilt the "number-one killer," surpassing cancer, heart failure, accidents, and addictions, because it contributes to all these physical problems. If we could overcome guilt, they argue, we would live longer, spare ourselves a great deal of distress, and enjoy healthier relationships.

What do people feel guilty about? Anything! We feel guilty about work, family, sex, money, food . . . you name it. We feel guilty about our likes and dislikes, our assets and deficits. We feel guilty about not spending more time with our children, about eating fatty foods, about getting angry, and about not calling and visiting our parents more often.

The list could go on and on. Some people feel guilty for feeling guilty. Others don't believe they feel guilty enough. People generate guilt in themselves and stimulate it in others.

GUILT GOES ON AND ON

In fourth grade my teacher, Mrs. Condon, took the class candlepin bowling—a game played with a slender bowling pin and a small ball—as a reward at the end of the school year. I stood impatiently in line with the rest of my classmates to pay a buck and a half and receive my shoes. When I reached the head of the line, however, they simply gave me my shoes and did not ask for the money. Eager to catch up with my buddies, I rushed to my assigned lane.

A few moments later, Mrs. Condon's voice came over the loud speaker: "Class, someone still needs to pay for his shoes. Whoever forgot, please come see me." The announcement dropped like lead on my heart. I knew I hadn't paid, but something kept me from confessing. I had the money in my pocket. But I went right on bowling as if I hadn't heard my teacher's request.

The guilt of not paying for my shoe rental troubled me deeply but, for whatever reason, I did not pay. To this day I wonder if Mrs. Condon knew it was I for whom she paid out of her own pocket. In my guilt-prone moments, I half expect her to tap me on the shoulder.

Guilt feelings will stalk their prey for years. Childhood misdeeds, years after others have long forgotten them, can still plague the heart and mind of the guilty party.

BALANCING AN EMOTIONAL CHECKBOOK

After dating Kirk for more than a year and a half, Wendy, a senior in college, decided to leave him for another young man. She ended her relationship with Kirk abruptly and with little concern for his feelings. "I didn't think it would matter that much to him, but he fell to pieces," she told me.

She went on to tell me how he became depressed and even suicidal as a result of their breakup. The tears rolling off Wendy's cheeks were visible signs of her feelings of guilt. She felt responsible for Kirk's pain.

Wendy, like everyone else who wrestles with guilt, felt indebted to the person she offended. She felt as though her emotional checkbook was out of balance, and she was in my office to find a way to get it balanced again.

The notion of indebtedness is closely linked with the root meaning of the word *guilt*. *Guilt* and *gold* come from the same Anglo-Saxon word *gylt*, meaning "to pay." When we feel guilty, we often feel that we must "pay" for our misdeed. However, trying to pay off our guilt is a futile endeavor. When Wendy, for example, tried to pay off her emotional debt to Kirk, she set an unconscious process in motion that caused her new boyfriend to dump her. "Having my boyfriend leave me was like getting kicked in the stomach," she told me. "Now I know how Kirk felt!"

In reality, Wendy's unconscious strategy was a roundabout way of kicking herself. Wendy tried to pay off her debt by suffering the same pain she had inflicted. And it worked—temporarily. She experienced freedom from guilt as long as she was being punished. But Wendy had never felt forgiven—by God, by Kirk, or by herself. Wendy drained her emotional account. She wrote the checks. But she continued to feel blackmailed by her feelings of guilt.

Guilt's torment is not appeased by writing checks. I often ask patients like Wendy: "How much more do you feel you will have to pay before the debt of guilt is fully paid off?" Their answer, like Wendy's, is nebulous. They don't know that their guilt feelings subject them to psychological blackmail. Every time they try to pay off their accuser, it calls for more.

WHAT IS GUILT?

Guilt comes in many forms. Social scientists talk about *objective* or legal guilt, which occurs when society's laws have been broken. The lawbreaker is guilty whether or not he feels sorry. *Social* guilt occurs when a person breaks an unwritten law of social expectation. *Personal* guilt occurs when a person compromises her personal standards. And *theological* guilt involves a violation of God's law.

When I was a graduate student earning two degrees, one in theology and one in clinical psychology,

I noticed that the professors in the two disciplines had very different perspectives on guilt. On the one hand, my theology professors talked about guilt as a *condition* that results from violating God's laws. On the other hand, my psychology professors defined guilt as a *feeling*.

Noting the difference, I decided with the help of my academic mentor, Archibald Hart, to survey pastors to find out how they understood guilt feelings. Did they see guilt as a positive force, or a negative one? Did they think guilt feelings came from God or from the devil? In our results, we found that few of the pastors had difficulty defining guilt as a theological condition, but most of them were confused about what to do with the *emotion* of guilt. And if *pastors* are confused about what to do with guilt feelings, imagine how confused their congregations must be!

As I worked on understanding the emotion of guilt, I began to see a difference between real guilt and false guilt, or as some say, good guilt and bad guilt. *Being* guilty differs from *feeling* guilty. Guilt is the state of having done a wrong or committed an offense. This is guilt as defined by theologians. But guilt also is the painful feeling of self-reproach resulting from doing wrong—guilt as defined by psychologists. *Real* guilt feelings result when we have done wrong. *False* guilt, however, seizes us when we believe we have done something wrong *when, in fact, we have done nothing wrong*.

True guilt keeps people in line by acting as an internal alarm that warns us of danger. False guilt, however, keeps the alarm ringing even after we've been notified of the problem or even when there is no danger. Compare the two alarms:

The true guilt alarm . . .

- is based on solid facts
- signals an objective condition
- is heard when the responsibility for wrongdoing is clear
- sounds as a result of a violation of a law, code, or moral value

The false guilt alarm . . .

- is based on personal feelings
- signals a subjective experience
- is heard when the responsibility for wrongdoing is not clear
- sounds in the absence of a violation of a law, code, or moral value

We do not need to give in indiscriminately to all of our feelings of guilt. If our guilt alarm is false, we need to turn it off and go on with life. But many of us run into trouble when we try to dismantle our false guilt. Like a car alarm triggered when the owner is away, false alarms go on and on and on. In fact, the ringing is so persistent that it often makes people behave as though the guilt were real.

GUILT'S MOST LETHAL FORM

This book is concerned primarily with guilt's most pervasive and destructive form—*irrational* or false guilt. Paradoxically, false guilt hits hardest those who deserve it least. Cindy, a woman in her mid-forties, suffered from feelings of guilt every time she tried to let down and relax. Finally her friends convinced her to join them for an afternoon on Santa Monica Beach. They marked their spaces with beach towels and settled in for a relaxing day in the sun. However, after fifteen minutes, Cindy's guilt alarm rang. *I am wasting my time here*, she thought. *I should be doing something worthwhile.* She made an awkward excuse about forgetting an assignment at home and left her friends in disbelief.

A man in his fifties told me about a golf game he had played as a young man. At the end of the round of golf he was handed a slip of paper, which he misread. It actually said, "How was your caddy today?" But he read it as, "How was your game today?" and scribbled the word, "Horrible!" He fell into deep guilt when he learned later that the slip was used as an evaluation of the caddy. "I thought I might have caused him to lose his job," he told me more than thirty years later. He had apologized to the caddy. He was profuse and emotional in his confession of misunderstanding the request to me. He talked about feeling guilty even now, knowing full well his mistake was innocent.

A French proverb says: "There is no conscience so soft as a clear conscience." Many good people live with a dysfunctional emotional immune system that does not protect them from the condition of undeserved guilt.

FALSE ACCUSATIONS

Often we struggle with false guilt because we don't understand the difference between true and false guilt.

I'll say it again: *Feeling* guilty differs from *being* guilty. For instance, if you were to steal a wristwatch from a jeweler, you would *be* guilty, whether you *felt* guilty or not. The laws of society and moral principles make this clear: stealing is against the law, and it is morally wrong. Being in a state of guilt is the direct result of being in violation of moral and civil law.

But *feeling* guilty doesn't mean a person *is* guilty. Feeling does not equal fact. It is not against God's moral law to enjoy a pleasant meal on vacation, even when a nagging inner voice says, "You don't deserve this." The same is true with any number of behaviors that disturb the conscience. Feeling guilty does not necessarily make you guilty.

Janet grew up in a family that demanded she be at the top of her high school class. However, when she entered college, she was competing with other students who had been at the top in their classes. For the first time, Janet was not the "best." Trying not to let down her parents, she drove herself beyond her reach. Then she punished herself by getting depressed, not sleeping well, and studying all weekend without taking time for fun.

A perceptive counselor helped Janet see that not being at the top of her college class was not a crime. Self-image was not tied to academic super-excellence. She learned there was no reasonable cause for the punishment she had been inflicting on herself. Her guilt alarm was false.

People doing battle with irrational guilt are distorting reality. This distortion probably stems from a long list of unspoken "shoulds"—indisputable, ironclad rules that they live by. Guilt-prone people are compelled to be someone they aren't, or they feel obligated to do something that does not objectively make sense.

Here are some of the most common and unreasonable shoulds:

- I should always feel loved and accepted by everyone all the time.
- I should be the epitome of generosity, courage, and unselfishness.
- I should never feel hurt.
- I should be the perfect friend, partner, spouse, and parent.
- I should be able to find a quick solution to every problem.
- I should be able to endure any hardship and difficulty with equanimity.
- I should understand and know everything.
- I should never feel anger or jealousy.
- I should never make mistakes.
- I should never get sick or even be tired.

The road to overwhelming guilt feelings is paved with an infinite variety of "shoulds." The sheer number of "shoulds" increases the chances of violations that produce guilt. By multiplying self-imposed rules, people are, in a sense, sowing the seeds of *oughts*, *musts*, and *shoulds*. These weeds grow out of control and destroy the good vegetation. Our minds, if filled with shoulds, can become an unkempt patch of irrational rules, obligations, and laws.

False guilt, unhealthy guilt, undeserved guilt, or irrational guilt is guilt at its worst. Undeserved guilt cripples good relationships. Unhealthy guilt is love's unseen enemy.

2

Coping with Guilt

This morning we are going to learn to juggle. Each of you should be holding three brightly colored scarves."

More than a thousand psychologists and physicians had gathered in the ballroom of the Disneyland Hotel for a conference on laughter. This morning we were listening to Dr. Steve Allen, Jr., the son of the famous comedian.

"I'm going to lead you through a dozen steps to teach you the fine art of juggling," he told us. "First, take one of your scarves, hold it out at arm's length, and drop it."

We couldn't believe our ears. "Drop it?" people murmured. You could feel the resistance. Nobody around me dropped a scarf. And I certainly wasn't going to fall for that trick.

"C'mon now drop it!" Dr. Allen commanded. One by one, we reluctantly released our scarves, and they fluttered to the carpeted ballroom floor.

"There now, doesn't that feel better?" asked Dr. Allen. "You have gotten your mistake over with. This is the first critical step in learning to juggle. We call it the guilt-free drop."

I could feel the tension roll off my shoulders. *I'm allowed to make mistakes*, I thought. *I don't have to be a perfect juggler*.

Everyone suffers from needless self-punishment. When we fall short of raising the "perfect" child, when we get a C on a test, when a colleague is promoted above us, we punish ourselves. Our internal tape recorder begins to say, "You are a terrible parent," "You are dumb," or "You are a loser."

Even the silliest of infractions fuels our guilt. A successful businesswoman came to see me because of her struggle with guilt. As a small girl she was taught to brush her teeth nightly. Occasionally she would fall into bed exhausted after a hard day. She would awaken suddenly in the middle of the night, panicked because she realized she had failed to brush. Arising, she'd stumble into the bathroom to ease the discomfort of her deeply ingrained feelings of guilt.

THE INNER COURTROOM

Each of us has a judge and jury inside. We are in the courtroom daily, waiting to hear the verdict: "Guilty or not guilty?" Not that the decision has any bearing on the truth. It is our emotions, not reality, that will determine the verdict. So we wait in lonely silence, hoping our bruised conscience is spared another blow.

The most wrenching pain, however, is not the pain of guilt. It is the pain of broken relationships—relationships destroyed by guilt.

Rick, a young husband, loved his wife but had trouble showing it. He seldom kissed her. Understandably, his wife read his refusal to kiss as a lack of love. Little did she know that years before, Rick had been taught by his mother that kissing was immoral. Intellectually he knew his mother was wrong and the idea silly. But he was unable to rid himself of his false guilt.

Most people recognize the gnawing feeling of guilt, but few recognize guilt's power to destroy relationships. After a decade of research and working professionally with countless individuals, couples, and families afflicted with guilt, I recognized a painfully evident truth: *The feelings of guilt silently undermine the human capacity for building healthy relationships.* Guilt undercuts our ability to love and corrupts our capacity to be authentic.

WAYS OF DEALING WITH GUILT

Unless we learn to deal with guilt effectively, we will never break free of its bondage. Typically, we will handle our feelings of guilt in one of four ways: (1) find someone to blame, (2) confess to everything, (3) confess just to make yourself feel better, and (4) confess and change your behavior because you are genuinely sorry. The first three options have their pitfalls and dangers—as we shall see.

Find Someone to Blame

When I was nine years old, I got a new pair of Hush Puppy shoes that I could not stand. I protested to my parents, but they insisted that I wear the shoes until they were worn out or I outgrew them.

Since I didn't foresee an immediate growth spurt, I decided to make my shoes wear out—fast! I walked my bike to the top of our steep asphalt street and coasted down the hill using the tips of my shoes as brakes. After an hour, I had worn a hole into the tip of both shoes. Triumphantly, I showed the worn-out shoes to my parents.

My parents were furious! To save my own hide, I lied and blamed my older brother. "Roger made me do it!" My parents, needless to say, were not impressed with my explanation.

Even though I've grown up, I still fall into the trap of blaming others for my own mistakes. Recently, I missed a live radio interview with my friend, Chuck Snyder. He had scheduled me weeks before and had been publicizing the interview on his program for days. But the afternoon of the interview Leslie invited me to run a few errands with her, and I agreed—not remembering that I was supposed to be in the studio.

At about 9:00 that evening I realized my mistake. I was mortified. And even though it was my responsibility to keep track of my own schedule, I blamed Leslie for my mistake. "I never miss appointments! Why didn't you remind me?" I asked Leslie. "I never would have missed the interview if you hadn't asked me to go on those crazy errands!"

Ever since Adam blamed Eve, and Eve blamed the

serpent, we have learned the trick of finding excuses and shifting blame. Accused of wrongdoing, we respond, "Who me?" "I didn't do it," "It's only a game," "Well, she asked for it," or "I didn't mean to."

Often blamers are highly critical people. I knew a crotchety man named Clifford who constantly criticized others in an attempt to shift the blame away from himself. If Clifford did not meet his weekly work quotas, he blamed his boss. If he was late for a meeting across town, he'd criticize the mayor for not building better roads. If he forgot to pick up the dry cleaning on his way home, his wife was to blame. If the preacher's sermon did not inspire him, the pastor was no good. Everyone was to blame except Clifford.

Laying the blame on others is our attempt to take the blame off ourselves and shed our feelings of guilt. But it seldom works. Because of his inability to take responsibility for his own mistakes, Clifford rarely held a job for more than a year. His marriage teetered on the brink of divorce. And he never enjoyed the comfort of a caring community. Attempts to escape guilt by blaming others only exaggerated his own guilt.

Confess to Everything

We love to wallow in our feelings, even when the wallowing is painful. And even when the wallowing involves guilt. Something about being found guilty brings relief. Admitting guilt takes the pressure off. Being found out is an escape valve for the guilty conscience.

Every time there is a well-publicized murder, innocent people "confess" to the crime. During the reign of the "Hillside Strangler," at least five people confessed to

being the murderer. People under the crushing weight of
emotional guilt are looking for any possible way out, even
false confessions. They are willing to purge themselves by
confessing to crimes they haven't done. My friend, Myrl
Carner, who has served as a detective in the Seattle
Police Department for more than twenty years, once told
me, "Some people are dying to be found guilty."

Paradoxically, there is something good about feeling bad. There is certainly something good about own-
ing up to misdeeds. But sometimes a guilt-prone person
will confess to things she did not do.

Confession is good for the soul, but false confession
causes relational chaos. I know a woman who could
win a blue ribbon for the originality and frequency of
her confessions. She takes full responsibility for any and
every unfortunate situation. She sees herself as responsible for bad weather ("I'm sorry about this rain, I
should have known better than to schedule a picnic in
late spring"), unexpected road construction ("Why
didn't I call AAA before we left home?"), or anyone's
disappointment about anything ("I'm so sorry, I would
do anything to make you feel better"). Her guilt is
boundless. Like Atlas, she carries the whole world on
her shoulders. She has caused such strife in her home
due to her compulsion for repeated confessions that in
a counseling session, her daughter said, "If Mom says
'I'm sorry' one more time, I'm going to explode!"

Some people get relief from their painful guilt feelings by accepting unconditional guilt. Even God can't
blame them since they already feel guilty for everything.
They have beat God and everyone else to the punch.

Admitting guilt on every count is actually a subtle
way of denying guilt for anything. The woman suffering

from confession-obsession would often tell her family, "I'll try to be better, but I'm only flesh and blood." She confessed her wretchedness continually, but she never went through the hard work of changing her behavior. Being "wretched"—resigning herself to a lifetime of self-condemnation—was her convoluted way of trying to get herself off the hook. But like those who blame others for their mistakes, she never experienced freedom from guilt. And her false confessions prevented genuine, intimate relationships from developing.

Confess Just to Make Yourself Feel Better

The common options for coping with feelings of guilt—blaming others or compulsively confessing—don't work. Surely there is another option.

Indeed, there is. The third option is to confess your pangs of guilt and change your behavior. However, while this option seems to be better than the others, it also has its pitfalls. Some people change their behavior simply to get guilt off their back and feel better about themselves. They care more about how they *feel* than what *kind* of person they are.

Say, for example, I forget my wife's birthday. I would feel like a heel and do almost anything to avoid feeling so terrible again. You can bet I wouldn't forget her birthday the following year. And when that day came, our celebration would look very similar to other years' celebrations. We would go to a nice restaurant, and I would give her a thoughtful gift. But this time I would be motivated to celebrate not by love, but by guilt. I would think, *No one can say Les Parrott didn't remember his wife's birthday this year!* My guilt would cut the meaning out of the loving gestures—and they would be simply that—gestures.

When the Israelites were slaves of the Egyptians, God sent numerous plagues to convince the pharaoh of his power and to force him to let the Israelites go. Time after time, Pharaoh promised to release the people if God would stop the plague, and time after time, Pharaoh reneged on his promise. Pharaoh cared more about taking away the pain of the plagues than he cared about his relationship with the one true God. His "confessions" and "repentance" were more manipulative than genuine.

Some of us act like Pharaoh. We change our behavior simply to get rid of the plague of guilt and feel better about ourselves—not to be better people. We confess our sins but never question our motives. And as T. S. Eliot said in his play, *Murder in the Cathedral*, "The greatest sin is to do all the right things for all the wrong reasons."

Confess and Change Your Behavior Because You Are Genuinely Sorry

We have looked at the ineffective ways of dealing with guilt: finding someone to blame, confessing to everything, or confessing just to make yourself feel better. Each of these techniques for dealing with guilt seems to work. After all, they help you cope with the pain of guilt. They seem to make you feel better. But in reality, these techniques destroy relationships.

The *only* effective way to deal with guilt is to confess and change your behavior because you are *genuinely* sorry for the pain your wrongdoing has caused. When you confess out of genuine sorrow, your focus will not be on yourself, but on the other person. You will worry less about your painful feelings of guilt and more about the pain you have caused the other person.

Sometimes, however, the process of repentance can seem so painful that we will do almost anything to avoid it. That was Katherine's problem.

I was assigned to counsel Katherine when she was brought to the hospital after a suicide hotline counselor reported her suicidal threats. Several months before, her family discovered that she had a brief affair with her sister's husband. Since that time Katherine, a single twenty-five-year-old woman, had gone into a depression.

When I talked to Katherine, however, she seemed more defensive than depressed, and I suspected that she was faking her depression. To help with my diagnosis, I had her take the Minnesota Multiphasic Personality Inventory, or the MMPI—a widely used true-and-false questionnaire with more than 500 questions. The test not only reveals possible psychological problems; it also is able to determine whether a person is lying.

In Katherine's case, she was. For nearly two months she had convinced her family and friends that she was severely depressed. But in reality, Katherine was wrestling with guilt more than depression. Guilt often masks itself as depression, but Katherine was *consciously* faking symptoms of depression to garner sympathy. Psychologists call this technique *malingering*. It is a way of avoiding responsibility. In Katherine's case, she was faking depression as a way of avoiding guilt for having an affair with her sister's husband.

Malingering is always a delicate therapeutic issue. And it is best to confront it with compassion rather than condemnation. I went over some of the test results with Katherine and then set the profile aside. "I suspect you are carrying a lot of pain inside," I told her. "I know you betrayed your sister, but we haven't talked about that yet. Are you close to her?"

"Yes. Well . . . " she paused. "I used to be."

"Tell me about the two of you."

"There's nothing to tell."

Katherine's eyes filled with tears. I remained quiet.

"Their marriage has always been on the rocks. Besides, it was only one time and he is the one who came on to me."

She seemed to be shifting the blame to her sister's husband. To clarify her thinking, I asked her, "You didn't want it to happen?"

"I don't know, I just know I'm sorry."

"Have you told your sister that?"

"I've done everything I know how to do, and it's just not enough." Katherine began crying, and I handed her a box of tissues. "I feel so overwhelmed, so defeated," she told me in an innocent tone. "I keep having the impulse to run away from it all."

"What keeps you from doing that?" I asked.

"What do you mean? Do you think I should run away?"

"Maybe you already have."

She looked at me. "Do you think I'm . . . " Katherine stopped and took a deep breath. I could almost see the wheels of her mind turning. "I have wanted to know it's not my fault, but . . . it is." Katherine began to sob. "I have wanted my sister and everyone else to see how much this whole thing has messed me up. It has. I've been a wreck."

"But?" I said slowly. I could sense that she was coming to a pivotal point of self-awareness and didn't want her to miss it.

"But I can't pretend any longer. I've got to come to terms with what I have done. I did betray my sister. She has a right to blame me. I betrayed myself too. I have replayed that night a thousand times and I would do anything to erase it."

The session was agonizing. Katherine's shoulders shuddered, her chin quivered, and she cried over the pain she had caused her sister.

I continued to see Katherine for a few more sessions. She eventually admitted that her suicide threats were a way of deflecting guilt, and she owned up to her part in a terrible relational tangle. Katherine achieved some sense of peace. I don't know if her sister ever forgave her. But I do know that Katherine owned up to her misdeed. She took responsibility for her actions and confessed her wrongdoing out of genuine sorrow. Her energy for living returned, and I began to see the authentic Katherine emerge.

The greater the pain of our guilt, the more we will be tempted to deal with it in unhealthy ways: blaming others, or, in this case, going even so far as to fake an illness to garner sympathy. If we have developed a healthy way of coping with guilt, however, we will recognize our fault, repent in sorrow for our behavior, and make changes that will restore our relationship with the person we have wronged. We will explore that process in more depth in Chapter 5 when we talk about godly sorrow. First, however, we must learn how to adjust our internal thermostat, the conscience.

3

Conscience: Your Internal Thermostat

Marilyn, a successful business owner, was taking her seven-year-old son to school after he missed the bus. Running late for an appointment, she hurriedly buckled the boy into his seat and raced to the freeway. As she pulled the car into the flow of traffic, the passenger door swung open. The child was thrown out into the path of an oncoming car and critically injured.

Marilyn literally screamed and cursed at herself for much of the day. She paced the floor of the hospital all night. Just before dawn, Marilyn shot herself with a pistol. Her child died the same morning. Marilyn's guilt, left unchecked, wreaked havoc on her, and on the lives of her husband and two surviving children.

One of my first patients, Matt, was a forty-year-old Vietnam vet. Matt was a patient in the psychiatric hospital of University of Southern California

Medical Center. He suffered from survival guilt—the guilt people experience when they make it through a tragedy and others do not. For two decades, Matt carried a burden of guilt so heavy that finally he snapped. One night, in a psychotic rage, he gouged out his right eye. With a butcher knife, he cut through his right leg below the knee, and in a final attempt at assuaging his guilt, he cut off his left hand. This was Matt's gruesome attempt to exorcise his demon of guilt.

How could guilt become so toxic? What would goad a mother of three into taking her own life? What would provoke a war veteran to inflict gruesome self-mutilation? Where does self-destructive guilt come from? Part of the answer is found in the human conscience.

Our conscience is the inner signal that lets us know what we *ought* to have been and what we *ought* to have done. A person with a "good" conscience is said to be scrupulous. The word *scruple* is derived from the Latin word *scrupulum*, which means a small pebble. If a small pebble gets lodged inside a person's shoe, he will feel pain. The scrupulous person feels the agony of real or imagined guilt. And the conscience may not know the difference between the two kinds of guilt.

Almost anything can prick a tender conscience: an overdue bill, an approaching police car, a collection plate, or a cool glance from the boss. As the hapless victim of needling oughts and shoulds, one is left wondering what the conscience is good for. Did God goof? I don't think so. But I do think we err in giving too much power to our conscience.

HOW DOES YOUR CONSCIENCE DEVELOP?

Once I asked a large group, "Who said, 'Let your conscience be your guide'?"

"The Bible," one man responded. Several other people nodded.

I shook my head. "The Bible doesn't say that," I corrected him. "Jiminy Cricket did!"

Contrary to popular opinion, the conscience in and of itself is not a reliable voice of God. Each person's moral fingerprints are unique. A psychopath may murder a relative and feel no guilt, whereas a shy recluse may feel overwhelmed with guilt for dialing the wrong number. However, the conscience *is* a gift from God that, properly trained, can help us make moral decisions. But because of sin, often the conscience is poorly trained. And the poorly trained conscience is faulty and can in no way be seen as the most reliable guide.

Babies, for example, are not born with the Ten Commandments, the Sermon on the Mount, and the laws passed by Congress imprinted on their minds. Nor are they born with an internal moral thermostat for automatically telling right from wrong. Rather, children must be taught right from wrong by their parents or other adult figures. To avoid punishment, gain rewards, or simply maintain their love, children accept their parents' standards of behavior. Each time a child hears "Stop that," "No, no," or "Naughty," her idea of what's right and what's wrong is strengthened, and her conscience begins to develop.

As the conscience develops, it slowly gains more

and more home rule. The inner sense of "oughtness" gains strength until the mature adult no longer relies entirely on parents, friends, preachers, or police to know what is right. Finally, each of us sets our own standards, and we reward or punish ourselves by what we think we deserve.

Unfortunately, many of us are harder on ourselves than other people are. To prove our independence, we declare our own rules and invite our conscience to show no mercy. The conscience then critiques our thoughts, wishes, and actions with unforgiving judgment. Almost without knowing it, we become legalists—more concerned about keeping rules than having healthy, loving relationships. That was the problem of Ron Stevens.

THE LEGALIST

Ron Stevens, an ex-Marine turned busy executive, sat in the tiny waiting room outside my office with three growing boys in tow: Paul, sixteen and stocky; Neil, fourteen and wiry; and Donny, eleven and wearing a Phillies cap. We all shook hands and exchanged awkward hellos. I led them into my office while Neil and Donny traded exaggerated panicked looks and gestures.

They sat down and Ron said to me, "Well, Doc, these boys can't seem to follow instructions."

"And that's why you're here?" I asked.

"They know the rules in our house, but they are bent on breaking them." The two older boys sat silent while Donny idly leafed through a small stack of baseball cards. "Give me those, son," Ron said and jerked the cards out of the boy's small hands. "See what I mean, Doc?"

I winced at Ron's insensitivity and the embarrassment he caused Donny. "Not exactly," I said.

"These boys need a good dose of discipline," Ron said.

We spent the rest of the session exploring their home life. I learned that Ron's wife died of cancer many years ago and that there was another son, Ron, Jr., who was eighteen and moved out on his own a few months earlier. Ron had not heard from his son since then. We wrapped up the session, and I scheduled the next appointment with the father alone.

A week had passed when Ron said, "Doc, I have lost a wife and my first son. I don't want to lose the rest of my boys."

We met for the next few weeks until Ron saw the painful truth: his emphasis on rules and discipline was driving away his boys. His legalistic insistence on their obedience was destroying their relationship.

The early church also struggled with legalism. Because Judaism emphasized keeping God's Law, the first Christians had to decide what place laws and rules would play in their new lives in Christ. In the book of Galatians, Paul goes to great lengths to convince new Christians that circumcision is not necessary for their salvation. Following the rules, keeping the old Jewish laws, will not save you. Only a relationship with Christ will bring you redemption.

When the conscience is overly scrupulous, law takes precedence over love, and relationships suffer. Perhaps because he had been a Marine, Ron raised his sons like they were in boot camp. Laws and rules have their place. Keep the law and we stay out of jail. Rules, in a sense, give us our freedom. But rules turn sour when they become more important than relationships. In Ron's case, his emphasis on rules was so strong that he drove away his oldest son and risked alienating his other three sons.

Relationships require more than adherence to the letter of the law. A clinical supervisor reviewing one of my early cases once told me, "Whenever you see excess scrupulosity, look out for emotional damage." After counseling numerous families burdened by an overactive conscience, I have seen her words ring true again and again. Legalism drains grace from a home. It kills joy in a church. Legalism finds rules for every situation. It breeds oppressiveness, judgment, and unforgiveness into persons and institutions.

THE AMORALIST

Bit by bit, the word leaked out: John, a trusted lay leader in the church, was having an affair with a woman from another church who worked in his office. The congregation reacted with shock and anger. The pastor and several elders visited John to confront him with his sinful behavior. But John was unrepentant. He saw nothing wrong with what he'd been doing. After all, he said, they were both adults, and they weren't hurting anyone. In fact, he felt he was spiritually stronger because of the intimacy he and his lover had enjoyed!

John is an amoralist. He has no sense of right or

wrong. Even though his affair destroyed two families, devastated a loyal wife and three children, and damaged his church, he refused to admit that he had done anything wrong.

People like John who have never developed an adequate conscience have *superego lacunae*, meaning "holes in the conscience." They perform all sorts of antisocial acts and suffer no remorse or guilt. For example, when Charlie Starkweather went on a cross-country shooting spree in the 1950s, killing fourteen innocent victims, he told a jury, "It was just like shootin' rabbits!"

However, the problem of a conscience with holes is not limited to sociopaths. Many experts believe society is breeding an unhealthy respect for "getting away with it." They point to the cheating epidemic that is sweeping America as a primary example. People are cheating because "everyone is doing it" or as a way of "getting even." We have almost grown accustomed to reading about business leaders, television evangelists, and government officials who have cheated, told bald-faced lies, and felt no pain of guilt.

THE HEALTHY CONSCIENCE

People with a healthy conscience seldom show up in my office, but I can remember a college student who came to me to clear her conscience—and changed her life as a result.

The first time Trudy showed up in my office, she refused to look at me. Her hair was shaggy and unkempt, and she wore a T-shirt and faded jeans that were far too tight for her large figure. Her supervisor from nursing school had recommended that Trudy see me, for she was failing every course and could not get along with the other nurses. But Trudy refused to open up to me.

After talking in circles for a while, I stopped the conversation. "I can understand why you don't feel like talking to me," I said. "But I doubt if things are going to improve if you refuse to talk about your problems."

She looked startled, but I continued. "Feel free to leave," I said. "But if there comes a time when you are willing to level with me, call for an appointment, and I'll be glad to see you."

She left, but a few days later she came back. And this time her attitude was different. She had come of her own volition. And she was ready to talk. This time she told me a long, sad story about an unsavory relationship with an older man who had taken advantage of her. As a result she was dying inside from the pain of guilt.

I listened carefully as she told her story. Then I told her she could be forgiven—that if she repented of her behavior, she could go on with her life and make changes for the better.

Six weeks later, Trudy's supervisor called me to report that the young woman had done a complete turnaround. "She is happy with school," the supervisor said. "Her classwork has improved considerably, and so have her relationships with the other students. She will be staying in school, and I believe she will graduate and make a fine nurse."

Trudy suffered from the pain of guilt, a pain no less severe than actual physical pain. But that pain is necessary to our survival, as Dr. Paul Brand demonstrates in his book *Pain: The Gift Nobody Wants*. In his work with lepers, Dr. Brand discovered that lepers were not able to feel pain in their extremities. Without the danger signal of pain, lepers repeatedly injured themselves. As a result, they lost their most vulnerable parts—their fingers and their toes.

Without the pain of guilt feelings, everyone would become moral lepers. But the pain of guilt in a healthy conscience keeps us from self-destructive acts. A healthy conscience tenses up whenever a wrong has been done, but it also eases and comes back to a relaxed state when a wrong has been corrected.

How does a healthy conscience function? A healthy conscience is not bound by rigid rules. It bends without breaking. Like the gyroscope on a ship, it adjusts to new situations. The person with a strong conscience lives by principles, is guided by an enlightened intellect, and is inspired to follow ideals. In addition, the person with a healthy conscience is discerning. He or she carefully thinks through moral problems and, in reaching a moral decision, balances a concern for rules with a deeper concern for relationships.

Here are other qualities that make up the healthy conscience.

1. A healthy conscience does not look for an easy way out.

During an exam, a proctor saw one student obviously cheating. When the exam was over and the students handed in their blue books, the proctor pulled the cheater aside. "I'll take that book, please," he said. "I saw you cheating."

The student stared the proctor in the eye. "Cheating? Me? Have you any idea who I am?"

"No," said the proctor.

"Good!" said the student, who grabbed a stack of blue books, threw them into the air with his own, and ran from the room.

Unlike this crafty student, people with a healthy conscience face up to their wrongdoing. They know when they have stepped out of line. They do not try to deny or excuse it, because the healthy conscience is not afraid of responsibility.

2. A healthy conscience accepts human weakness.

One of the most celebrated of all "I Love Lucy" episodes featured Lucy wrapping candy as it passed on a conveyor belt. In the mistaken belief that Lucy was handling the candy with competence, her supervisor doubled the conveyor belt's speed. An occasional piece of candy got wrapped, but most of them ended up in her mouth or hidden in her blouse.

The unhealthy conscience is like Lucy's supervisor, who ignored her limits and relentlessly increased her demands. An unhealthy conscience pushes the limits of our humanness and eventually breaks our spirits.

The healthy conscience, on the other hand, accepts human limits and adjusts its expectations to fit them. For example, a woman who locks her keys in the car may feel stupid, but she will not grovel in her mistake. Instead, her healthy conscience will help her to analyze the offending act or word, control the damage, and then move on with life.

3. A healthy conscience is concerned with "morality" and not with "moralism."

People with unhealthy consciences are more concerned with looking good than being good. They are moralists who always tell everyone else what is right and what is wrong. Because they are so preoccupied with the rules of the road, they don't pay attention to the ideals and reasons behind the rules, nor do they have time to extend love and understanding to others.

People with healthy consciences, in contrast, know why something is right or wrong. Their actions are not based on rules, but on what is right and virtuous. They are easy to live with, affirming in their relationships, and always ready to show loving kindness.

4. A healthy conscience knows how to receive forgiveness.

The British poet William Cowper, well known as one of the principal writers of gospel hymns during the eighteenth century, penned the often sung words of God's mercy and forgiveness:

> There is a fountain filled with blood,
> Drawn from Emmanuel's veins,
> And sinners plunged beneath that flood
> Lose all their guilty stains.
>
> E'er since, by faith, I saw the stream,
> Thy flowing wounds supply,
> Redeeming love has been my theme,
> And shall be till I die.

Ironically, after a life riddled with loss, bouts of depression, and a suicide attempt, Cowper became convinced he was beyond forgiveness and even came to consider himself, "Damned below Judas." Not even his close friend the Reverend John Newton, author of "Amazing Grace," could convince Cowper of his redemption. Cowper died believing he was beyond forgiveness, though his hymns were used, among other things, in an influential campaign against slavery.

A tyrannical conscience has great difficulty accepting forgiveness. It demands additional punishment and tries to earn God's love. But God doesn't require us to pay our own way. He sent Jesus to cover for us, as Paul reminded the Galatians when he wrote: "Are you now trying to attain your goal by human effort? Have you suffered so much for nothing?" (Gal. 3:3–4). A healthy conscience knows how to receive forgiveness.

Before we take a closer look at guilt and how to control its influence on our lives, we need to answer one more question: What's shame got to do with guilt?

4

What's Shame Got to Do with It?

Shortly after midnight on Saturday, April 26, 1986, a power surge raced through reactor number four of the Chernobyl nuclear power plant. The reactor exploded, and for ten days a toxic nuclear cloud hovered over vast areas of the Soviet Union and Europe.

This nuclear disaster was the worst in history, producing ninety times the radioactive fallout of the atomic bomb dropped on Hiroshima and one million times the emission level at Three Mile Island. On a humanitarian assignment with World Vision International, I witnessed firsthand the devastation of this explosion. I saw ghost villages, gardens of weeds, and people physically mutilated by radiation. But the landscape and faces I witnessed, horrible as they were, were not as scarred as the human hearts I encountered.

Shortly after being picked up at the airport, my driver brought me to a building where nine feeble men awaited my arrival. They were the "liquidators," the brave Russian firefighters who had fought the initial reactor blaze and survived. While their bodies were filled with disease, it was their spirits that cried out for healing, and I was there to lead them in group therapy.

Each of these men told their story of combating the disaster and how they have tried to live with the consequences ever since. Breathing through artificial inhalers, their raspy voices let me in on what scorching heat and toxic fumes can do to the spirit as well as the body. But they also confessed a surprising burden. "We could not save our country from the pain," one of the men groaned.

"He is right," another said. "If we could have done more, perhaps others would have been spared."

Shocked, I said, "But you are heroes!"

I tried unsuccessfully to make eye contact. None of them looked at me. They stared blankly into nowhere or watched the floor.

"How has your country honored you for your heroism?" I asked.

One man spoke up. "With sickness. They honored us with sickness."

This lack of appreciation, coupled with their own self-imposed guilt over the fire that roared out of control, led these men to carry the dead weight of shame. If they had done a better job, they reasoned, their efforts would have been recognized and rewarded. But since they received inhalers instead of medals, they felt their shame deeply.

SHAME: THE CHERNOBYL OF THE SPIRIT

There comes a point when the emotional pain of guilt turns as toxic as any fumes in Chernobyl. When guilt moves from a thud-in-the-gut feeling to a feeling of failure, the seeds of shame are sown. When guilt seeps into the emotional bloodstream, permeating a person's sense of self-worth, guilt becomes shame. Shame is a spin-off from guilt. We may feel *guilty* for what we *did*, but we feel *ashamed* of who we *are*.

Shame is the Chernobyl of the spirit, and its fall-out contaminates the soul. Not satisfied to tinker with how we feel about ourselves, it changes who we are. Shame is not a gap between how we act and how we think we ought to act. It is the gulf between who we are and who we think we ought to be. It is not the feeling that we have done wrong. It is the feeling that we, our very *selves*, are wrong.

Each year I take my psychology students to prison to talk with men who have been diagnosed as sociopaths. When we arrive at the prison we pass through several iron doors and then through highly sensitive metal detectors. Eventually we arrive in a holding area where a metal gate closes electronically with a loud clang behind us. For the next three hours, my students experience life as a condemned person.

At the end of their visit my students understand that people who are condemned do not simply believe they have *done* something bad; they believe they *are* bad. In fact, one of the prisoners even had "born loser" tattooed on his arm.

People don't have to be in prison to feel shame.

All of us have difficulty separating who we are from what we do. An act of incompetence or poor form can trigger a shame reaction akin to the feeling of being caught outside with only our underwear on. But people who are especially prone to shame live with a deep sense of unworthiness and with the constant fear of rejection. Their fear about their worth is as frightening as any death sentence.

SHAME AND GUILT

In theory, guilt and shame are distinct. According to Freud, we feel *shame* when we fall short of our "ego ideal"—when we compromise our personal standards of who we ought to be. However, we feel *guilt* when we do something we know is wrong. While shame is the fear of *abandonment*, guilt is the fear of *punishment*. In other words, guilt results from crossing a boundary and being on the wrong side, while shame is the feeling of having been born there.

Freud may have been able to make theoretical distinctions between shame and guilt, but in reality, the two feelings often overlap. Guilt is mostly about things we have *done*. We feel guilty when we lie about our past, when we cheat on our diet, or when we commit adultery. And when we experience guilt for too long—when we begin to define who we are by what we have done—our guilt turns into shame. And shame strikes at our very identity, causing us to hate ourselves and to believe we are worthless.

Recently I counseled a middle manager who had lost his job. Already suffering from guilt because he had neglected his family during his busy years at work, he now felt a deep sense of shame because he was unable to find a new job. He told me, "If I can't find a job with all of my education and experience, there must be something dreadfully wrong with me." His long-standing guilt had turned into a crippling sense of shame.

TESTING YOUR LEVEL OF SHAME

"Shame on you; you know better than that."

"You ought to be ashamed of yourself for letting us down."

"After all we've done for you, how could you hurt us this way?"

Statements like these are all it takes to increase poor self-esteem and generate shame. If you grew up in an environment peppered by statements like these, you are probably troubled with feelings of shame as an adult.

The following test can help you assess whether your feelings of guilt have turned to shame. There are no right or wrong answers. Take as much time as needed. Answer each item carefully and accurately by placing a number beside each of the items as follows:

1 Rarely or none of the time
2 A little of the time
3 Some of the time
4 A good part of the time
5 Most or all of the time

_____ I feel I am not what I ought to be.

_____ I feel as if God must be disgusted with me.

_____ I feel as if I will never be acceptable.

_____ I feel flawed or blemished inside.

_____ I feel inferior to most people I know.

_____ I feel not only that I have made mistakes but that I am a mistake.

_____ I feel as if I just cannot measure up to the person I was created to be.

_____ I feel I can be a better person than I am but fear I'll never measure up.

_____ I feel I let people in my life down.

_____ I feel like a raunchy person.

_____ I feel rotten inside.

_____ I feel worthless.

_____ I feel nobody could really love me if they really know me.

_____ I feel like a phony.

_____ I feel humiliated.

_____ I feel that if people really know me they would never befriend me.

_____ My life will forever be dishonored by things in my past.

_____ I know others think poorly of me.

_____ If a person looks down on me I think they are right.

_____ My value is diminished because of my past.

_____ I feel hopeless.

_____ I make the same mistakes over and over.

_____ I feel that I'd like to change but can't.

_____ I feel inferior.

_____ I give up easily.

_____ I am disgusted with myself.

_____   I feel some things have basically ruined my life.

_____   I feel I am an immoral person.

_____   I feel I will never have a wonderful life.

_____   I feel lonely.

_____   I feel inadequate.

_____   I feel like a phony.

This test is scored by totaling the numbers on the items and subtracting 25. This gives a potential range of scores from 0 to 100. Although this test is not a failproof diagnostic tool, it will help you measure the intensity of your shame feelings.

Total   _____

                -25

              _____

Score   _____

80–100 You are in an extremely dangerous and toxic shame-zone. You are in serious need of professional help and should seek psychotherapy as soon as possible.

60–79 You may not be in immediate need of professional help, but you are not out of the danger zone. You could benefit from the assistance of a professional counselor who can help you process your struggle with shame at a personal level.

40–59 You are suffering from shame, which has probably taken its toll on you and the people around you. However, you are in a good position to learn how to escape shame's scourge.

20–39 You are on your way to escaping shame's clutches. Your episodes of self-loathing shame are temporary and you are not allowing your shame to get the best of you. However, you can benefit from some fine tuning with a compassionate listener.

0–19 You are free from shame's damage and have what it takes to build a solid foundation of healthy relationships. You will want to be aware of how you can help others who are suffering from shame.

There are always dangers in pinpointing an emotion and measuring its intensity. Use this self-test as a mirror to view your shame-proneness, but remember that it only reflects a single dimension. To more accurately understand the impact of shame on relationships, we must explore the roots of shame.

THE DEEP ROOTS OF SHAME

For most of us, the roots of shame lie buried deep in our childhood. As Dr. Missildine, a psychiatrist and researcher, found, we derive our self-worth as a child from only four or five people: our mother, father, brother or sister, close relative, neighbor, or teacher.[1] The way these people listen to us, treat us, and talk to us all affect how we see ourselves. By the time we have reached our early teens, we have learned very well that we are beautiful or ugly, smart or dumb, fast or slow, can spell or cannot, hate arithmetic or love it. Sometime between the years of thirteen and fifteen this mental picture of ourselves becomes complete.

What happens to this inner picture of ourselves as

we grow older? Does our picture of ourselves as children fade away? No. In fact, we will keep this picture in our minds for the rest of our lives. To be sure, as we mature into adulthood, we will begin to wrap that inner child with the trappings of adulthood: education, families of our own, careers. But underneath all the trappings of adult sophistication lies our self-concept. We may be six feet tall, sitting behind an important desk, or have the figure of a fashion model, but down in our psyche we are dominated by the attitudes we acquired as children.

Our original mental picture of ourselves, as Dr. Missildine suggests, is the work of all the people whose opinions influenced how we saw ourselves. But these people may have been wrong. They may have labeled us as slow or stupid. They may have disciplined us too harshly, or they may have not disciplined us enough. They may have even abused us verbally, emotionally, physically, or sexually. And their mistreatment damaged us to the point where we began to feel a deep sense of shame for being who we are.

None of us can emerge from childhood without feeling defective somehow. But if you are relentlessly hounded by shame, the roots of your struggle can invariably be traced to the inner child of your past, who did not receive the proper love and care needed to form a strong self-image.

Obviously, you cannot change what happened to you as a child. But the next two chapters will show you how to deal with guilt before it turns into crippling shame, and the rest of the book will give you tips for recognizing the effects of shame and for improving your relationships with friends, coworkers, spouse, parents, and children. Before moving ahead, however, let's look at the side effects of shame and expose shame's most debilitating lie.

THE SIDE EFFECTS OF SHAME

Shame can emotionally destroy us. The following are some of the most common problems associated with shame.

Feelings of Inadequacy

A friend showed me a cartoon of two cows in a pasture watching as a milk truck passes by. On the side of the truck are the words, "Pasteurized, homogenized, standardized, Vitamin A added." One cow sighs and says to the other, "Kinda makes you feel inadequate, doesn't it?"

Like the cows, shame-prone people feel a deep sense of inadequacy that eats away at their self-worth. Their feelings of inadequacy expand into feelings of inferiority and worthlessness. Shame-prone people begin to discount their own value.

Feelings of Rejection

Zola Budd, the eighteen-year-old South African woman who was selected to represent Great Britain in the 1984 Olympics, knows rejection. She was competing in a race against American Mary Decker when an accident knocked them both out of the running.

"We were around the curve and into the stretch,"

Zola Budd told reporters. "I was in front of Mary Decker and held the lead, feeling secure. Suddenly from behind I felt pain as spikes raked down the back of my left heel. I fought for balance and saw Mary falling to the track." Zola went on to tell how she didn't realize what had happened. "I didn't think I had done anything wrong. All I knew was that she had fallen from behind me."

The crowd in the stadium didn't agree. "The booing came down like a tidal wave of hostility," Zola said. "It was all aimed at me, and I realized that all of these people were blaming me for Mary Decker's problem. I came in seventh when it was over. All I wanted to do was find out what had happened to Mary."

Zola sought out Mary in the entrance tunnel. "I walked straight over to her and said the words that I wanted to get out the moment it happened. 'I'm sorry!' I said. 'I'm sorry. I'm sorry.' She looked at me, and she said, 'Get out of here. Get out! Just go. I won't talk to you!' Despite everything that everyone had said to me, I now thought that I was to blame."[2]

Zola Budd was not guilty of tripping Mary Decker. Yet, because Mary rejected her, she felt a deep sense of shame.

Feelings of Emptiness

Anne Morrow Lindbergh, in her enchanting book, *Gift from the Sea*, writes, "When one is a stranger to oneself, then one is estranged from others too. If one is out of touch with oneself, then one cannot touch others. . . . Only when one is connected to one's core is one connected to others."[3]

Shame cuts the core out of our being. Several authors have written on "the impostor phenomenon"—the belief that you do not deserve your success and that someday you will be exposed as a fraud. Often successful people have such a deep sense of shame that they put on masks to hide their hurt. Instead of shielding them, the masks only serve to make them feel like phonies.

Feelings of Loneliness

German theologian Paul Tillich said, "Language has created the word *loneliness* to express the pain of being alone, and the word *solitude* to express the glory of being alone." Shame robs people of the joy found in solitude, and it fills people with painful feelings of desperate aloneness.

For many people, loneliness is a serious personal problem, but because of shame, they do not have the strength that they need to risk reaching out to people. They do not want to risk rejection, and so they withdraw. Even people who are socially active may keep their emotional distance in order to lessen the risk of rejection. As a result, they too suffer loneliness.

Feelings of Dependency

Thomas Merton said that the person "who fears to be alone will never be anything but lonely." The loneliness of shame fosters unhealthy dependency—what has been called "codependency." Instead of needing people in a healthy way—to love and be loved—shame-based people need others in order to avoid being alone. They unwittingly become overly dependent in their

relationships as an antidote for shame and from fear of
rejection.

Shame-based people will often feel inadequate,
rejected, empty, lonely, and dependent. They may pity
themselves, be passive, withdraw, and lose their creativity. All of these side effects are obviously cause for
concern, but shame's greatest damage comes as a result
of a single lie.

SHAME'S LOOMING LIE

The greatest lie lived by a shame-prone person is
one that says, "I cannot change." Shame has a way of
bullying people into a dead end with no exits. The
shameful lie within them says, "I am what I am and
there is nothing I can do about it."

For his entire professional life, Martin Seligman at
the University of Pennsylvania has been studying what
makes people stop trying to change. As a twenty-one-
year-old graduate student fresh out of college, he
observed an experiment that set him on a quest for
unraveling why some people give up while others overcome.

In the experiment dogs were subjected to a minor
shock, which they could avoid by jumping over a low
wall that separated two sides of a shuttle box. Most
dogs learned this task easily. But other dogs just lay
down whimpering, with no will to try. When Martin
investigated the dogs who had given up, he found that
they had been used in a prior experiment in which
they received shocks no matter what they did. These
dogs had "learned" helplessness. Because they had

been given shocks regardless of whether they struggled or jumped or barked or did nothing, they learned that nothing they did mattered. So why try?[4]

Like the dogs in this experiment, people who are burdened with heavy doses of guilt and shame also have learned to be helpless. Because they believe that what they do makes no difference in what happens to them, they decide to give up.

During the Holocaust, many prisoners in the Nazi concentration camps also were in an apparently hopeless situation. But, as the psychiatrist Viktor Frankl observed, the prisoners who struggled to survive, who fought back against their captors, who refused to give up hope—those were the Jews who survived. But the Jews who gave up their will to live sickened and died quickly.[5]

Many things in life are beyond our control—eye color, race, the earthquakes in Southern California—but shame is not one of them. No one needs to live under the awful burden of shame. Instead, you can choose to change the way you think—especially the way you think about yourself.

Up till now, we have been diagnosing and defining the problems of guilt and shame. In the next chapters we will prescribe the remedies for healing these deadly diseases of the soul.

5

Godly Sorrow

Early Catholic guides for priests taking confessions warned about a type of person called "the scrupulous," people who held on to guilt no matter what. They were "unrelieved confessors" who, in spite of all assurances, could not accept grace.

If you are "scrupulous," if you are holding on to your guilt like a security blanket, there is a better way. Not only can you know God's grace, but you can *experience* it. The way to rid yourself of real guilt is through the path of godly sorrow.

Long ago, Paul had to write a letter to the Corinthians chastening them for their sins. When they responded by repenting and changing their behavior, he wrote:

> Even if I caused you sorrow by my letter, I do not regret it. Though I did regret it—I see that my letter hurt you, but only for a little while—yet now I am happy, not because you

were made sorry, but because your sorrow led
you to repentance. For you became sorrowful
as God intended and so were not harmed in
any way by us. Godly sorrow brings repentance that leads to salvation and leaves no
regret, but worldly sorrow [guilt] brings death.
(2 Cor. 7:8–10)

While guilt and sorrow are sometimes seen as the same
emotional experience, they could not be further apart.
Sorrow, unlike guilt, does not wallow in self-punishment and self-abasement. Instead, it is grounded in a
deep concern for relationships and constructive
change. Sorrow's focus, outlook, and, most impor-
tantly, its results, are radically different from the focus,
outlook, and results of the emotion of guilt. While sorrow results in positive, life-affirming changes, guilt
results in the destruction of self and relationships.

Consider the following eight distinctions between
godly sorrow and guilt.

1. Godly sorrow focuses on the other person.

Guilt is a selfish emotion. When people feel guilty
they focus on themselves exclusively. Their pains from
guilt are so great that they cannot begin to acknowledge the pain of the people they have hurt.

Godly sorrow, in contrast, allows people to look
beyond their own pain and enter the world of the person they have offended. For example, the prophet
Nathan tricked David into identifying with his victim
when he told the story of the rich man who stole the
beloved lamb of a poor man. Enraged by the incident,

David declared, "As surely as the LORD lives, the man who did this deserves to die! He must pay for that lamb four times over, because he did such a thing and had no pity" (2 Sam. 12:5–6).

But Nathan turned to David and said, "You are the man! ... You struck down Uriah the Hittite with the sword and took his wife to be your own" (2 Sam. 12:7, 9).

For the first time David realized what he had done to his victim, Uriah. He did not focus on himself. He did not say, "I'm the king—I can do whatever I want." Nor did he blame Bathsheba for seducing him. Rather, he acknowledged his sin against Uriah, confessed it to God, and was forgiven (2 Sam. 12:1–24).

2. Godly sorrow recognizes pain as a part of the healing process.

For the past two years I have worked on call as a medical psychologist in the burn unit of the University of Washington Medical Center. I have observed burn patients endure inhuman pain all in the hope of healing. I have watched them painfully exercise tender limbs with the guidance of a caring rehabilitation therapist. These patients have accepted the fact that healing comes only through pain. However, I have also worked with burn patients who refused physical therapy. Their highest priority was not to heal, but to avoid pain.

The feelings of guilt and sorrow work much the same way. Sorrow looks beyond the pain of the moment to the greater goal of healing a broken relationship. It cares about making a wrong right. Self-absorbed guilt, on the other hand, refuses to go through the pain required to heal a relationship.

3. Godly sorrow looks forward to the future.

Years ago a small town in Maine was proposed for the site of a great hydro-electric plant. Since a dam would be built across the river, the town itself would be submerged. However, out of fairness, the people were given several years to arrange their affairs and relocate.

Because of this decision, the town council canceled all improvements. No one repaired or painted buildings, roads, or sidewalks. Day by day the whole town got shabbier and shabbier. A long time before the flood waters came, the town looked uncared for and abandoned, even though the people had not yet moved away. One citizen explained: "When there is no faith in the future, there is no power in the present."

People troubled by feelings of guilt do not care about or plan for the future. Obsessed with the history of their failures, they cry futilely over situations that cannot be changed. Instead of driving with their eyes on the road ahead of them, they continually look behind them. But with their eyes focused on the rearview mirror, they cannot drive straight—and so they cause yet another accident.

Constructive sorrow, on the other hand, looks to the future. It keeps the eye trained on the road ahead, with only quick glances behind to prevent accidents.

In graduate school I worked for a short time in a treatment center for senior adults. One of my patients, Madeline, was almost ninety. Her husband, a decorated major in the U.S. Air Force, had passed away three years before. Madeline's room at the center was filled with memorabilia. Travel souvenirs and photos of deceased friends decorated her walls and shelves. But

on her ninetieth birthday, Madeline took down most
of the mementos from her past and replaced them with
pictures of places and things she wanted to learn
about. "You might think I've gone crazy," she told us.
"But I just want to start living again, and I've got to
start thinking about my future."

Madeline turned her back on the sunset and
smiled her welcome to the sunrise. Godly sorrow is the
same way. It helps people turn their back on the past
and start planning their future. Sorrow does not obsess
over the way things might have been. It does not revel
in regrets. Sorrow envisions what life can become and
believes it will be better than the past.

4. *Godly sorrow is motivated by our desire to change and grow.*

People who are plagued by feelings of guilt will do
anything to make themselves feel better. But often
their attempts at change do not last long. As soon as
they feel the burden of guilt lift, they are back to their
old destructive patterns of behavior. Constructive sorrow, on the other hand, is motivated by our desire to
make needed changes in our behavior and attitude.

I grew up in a church that sponsored old-fashioned
revivals. For more than a week, an evangelist would
come in to preach every day, in the morning and in
the evening. And normally, at the end of each service,
people would come forward to the altar and repent of
their sins. After a time, I noticed that often the same
people would kneel at the altar in successive services.

Why would people need to confess their sins over
and over again? The answer is simple. What do you
want more than anything else when you are loaded

with guilt? You look for a place to leave it. So, instead of changing the behavior that leads to your guilt, you go forward and "leave it at the altar." Released from your burden of guilt, you then fall back into your old patterns of behavior. Your "repentance" takes away your painful guilt, but it does not cure your problem.

Guilt brings us back to where we began in an endless cycle of bad behavior and shallow repentance. Godly sorrow, on the other hand, motivates us to make long-lasting changes that, although painful, can break the cycle of guilt and sinful behavior.

5. Godly sorrow is a choice; it is not coerced.

God knows that a genuine confession is rarely coerced. Through friends, spouses, counselors, Scripture, or his Spirit he gently leads us to a realization of our wrongdoings, then enables us to confess our sins and change our behavior.

Remember the story of the woman caught in adultery (John 8:2–11)? One morning, while Jesus was teaching in the courtyard of the temple, a group of Pharisees and teachers of the law burst in dragging a woman behind them. "Teacher, this woman was caught in the act of adultery!" they shouted. "The law says we are to stone such a woman. What do you say?"

There was deathly silence. Everyone waited to hear his answer. Jesus knew they were trying to trick him: if he said to stone her, he would be disobeying the Roman law, which forbade carrying out the death sentence. But if he told them not to stone her, he would be disobeying God's law. Jesus bent down and wrote in the sand. When the men continued to pester him, he said, "If any of you is without sin, throw the first stone!"

The angry little mob fell silent and stole away, one by one. The trembling woman and Jesus were left standing together.

"Where are they? Has no one condemned you?" he asked her.

"No one."

Jesus brushed the dirt from his hands. "Then neither do I condemn you," he told her. "Go now, and leave your life of sin."

I've often wondered if Jesus made a mistake when he said that. I mean, shouldn't he have gotten her to promise to change *before* pronouncing his forgiveness? But that's not Christ's way of responding to guilt. Jesus did not want a coerced confession motivated by fear. He wanted her to *choose* a better way of living in order to *be* a better person.

6. *Godly sorrow relies on God's mercy.*

Often we tend to feel that we must earn God's favor. When Martin Luther was still a Catholic monk, he struggled with unbounded feelings of guilt. He meticulously observed all the requirements of his religious order and confessed his sins repeatedly. He was so obsessed with confessing even the minutest sins that once his superior chided him: "If you expect God to forgive you, come in to confession with something to forgive!"

When we relate to God out of a guilty conscience, we try to earn our worth by being severely critical of ourselves. Rather than relying on God's mercy, we struggle to show God how good we are. A sense of inadequacy drives us to prove that we are deserving of God's forgiveness.

Godly sorrow, on the other hand, allows us to fully accept and experience God's forgiveness. When Martin Luther came across Romans 1:17, "the righteous will live by faith," he saw the futility of all his good works. For the first time, he recognized the futility of trying to earn God's acceptance, and he rested in the gift of God's amazing grace. His decision to base his life on faith changed his life and revolutionized the church.

7. Godly sorrow gives us a positive attitude.

As a college freshman, I took a two-week wilderness expedition in the Coast Mountains of British Columbia. My guide, a man named Fraiser, was a sturdy man with a beard and wire-rimmed glasses who was at least fifteen years older than I. Looking at him, I thought I wouldn't have any trouble keeping up. After all, I was a cocky college student.

After a mere three days on my mountain journey, however, my hip bones were rubbed raw from the padded belt on my thirty-pound backpack. My feet were covered with open blisters, and my legs were as stiff as tent poles. I could hardly climb another step while Fraiser, whose pack was twice the size of mine, whistled a happy tune as he all but skipped up the path.

"I don't understand it," I finally blurted out. "I'm no slouch. How can you do this so easily while every step I take hurts from the waist down?"

Smiling, Fraiser handed me his canteen. "Because you approach this mountain the same way you approach college. You see it as a test. You have made the mountain your enemy and have set out to defeat it.

Naturally, the mountain fights back. By the way it looks, it's winning!"

He laughed and continued walking. Only a few steps later I found myself whistling with Fraiser. The blisters still hurt, but I was gradually beginning to enjoy the journey. With each step higher I felt the sun warming my head and the thin mountain air filling my lungs. I was seeing trees and breathing deeply the scent of pine needles. I began to look at the mountain as a friend, not as an enemy. As a friend, the mountain lifted me and carried me along.

When we feel guilty, we have a negative attitude toward ourselves. We work to control and defeat guilt, and as a result, the spiritual aches and pains thrive. But when we feel godly sorrow, we maintain respect for ourselves. We do not try to conquer the self as much as we try to empower it to continue the journey. Instead of becoming our own enemy, we treat ourselves with respect, as we would a beloved friend.

8. *Godly sorrow results in real and lasting change.*

Constructive sorrow results in a true life change while guilt, at best, spins us into a cycle of temporary change followed by more self-condemnation.

I can almost hear some of you saying, "But feelings of guilt do motivate me to change my behavior." I agree. Guilt can lead to confession and change, but only in the short run. Motivation by guilt doesn't last. Life is a cross-country run, not a hundred-yard dash. Confession of guilt, in the absence of godly sorrow, short-circuits any attempt to make long-lasting life changes. The cycle looks like this:

Some entrepreneurs have turned this endless cycle of guilt feelings into a lucrative 900 phone business. A soothing female voice comes on the line: "Have you ever done something you feel bad about? Call me at Phone Confessions to leave your own message. Tell someone how you feel or tell someone that you're sorry."

As many as 14,000 people call in every day to confess or apologize on this computerized phone line. Others simply call to listen to the recordings of confessions by other people. Callers pay two dollars for the first minute and forty-five cents for each additional minute to eavesdrop on people baring their souls. Apparently just listening to confessions, finding solace in the fact that there are others who feel bad about ill deeds, helps some people deal with their guilt feelings. Not surprisingly, most of the money on this line is made from people who call repeatedly.

Some people relate to God as if he were an automated confessional. They confess as a way to "get God off their backs," rather than as a means of empowerment for actual change in their behavior and attitude.

SUMMARY

Dr. Bruce Narramore, professor of psychology at the Rosemead School of Psychology, teaches about the importance of godly sorrow in his book, *No Condemnation.*[1] The following figure is adapted from Dr. Narramore's work and may help you understand the stark contrast between guilt feelings and godly sorrow.

	Guilt Feelings	Godly Sorrow
Focus	on one's self	on the person offended
Outlook	toward the past	toward the future
Motivation	to avoid painful feelings	to change and grow
Attitude toward God	I can do it alone	I need your help
Attitude toward self	frustration	respect
Result	temporary change or stagnation	progressive change that lasts

MAKING HEALTHY CHOICES

Gerald, twenty-six years old, came to see me about a persistent problem with depression. He told me that his struggle began when he was nineteen, about the same time he took his faith more seriously and became more active in his church. He told me about his regular times of sadness and self-pity. "God must hate me," he wailed. "I let him down all the time. I'm a failure and don't deserve his love."

After some gentle probing, Gerald broke down and confessed that his real struggle was sexual. The weekend before he came to see me, he went on a date with a young woman from his church. After a movie and dinner, they drove to her apartment, and despite his determination not to get involved sexually, he couldn't resist her advances.

Gerald's "depression" did not originate in a chemical imbalance or from a grievous loss. His sadness was a mask for feelings of guilt that resulted from numerous, successive sexual encounters. "I've promised God I won't let myself get carried away like that," he said, "but I always end up failing him."

Gerald feels guilty, but he does not want to give up his sexual behavior. He carries a heavy burden of guilt, but it does not move him to be different. In fact, his guilt is what keeps him stuck. As long as he wallows in guilt he is refusing God's grace, and his sexual trysts will remain a part of his life.

Gerald has all the signs of being entrenched in unhealthy guilt. His guilt feelings are doing nothing to help him change. His focus is self-centered. He is obsessed with his past. He cares more about the pain he is feeling than about the pain he causes his women friends. He is trying to earn his worth rather than accept God's grace. And above all, he has replaced his self-respect with frustration and anger.

Gerald does not yet realize he has a choice. He has determined that his guilt alarm is not false. But he is not aware of the choices he can make for the better. He can choose to focus on the future. He can choose to accept God's grace. And he can choose to make real and lasting changes in his behavior.

Every guilt alarm presents us with a choice. First, we decide if the warning is true or false. Next, if we know our feelings of guilt are the result of an act of wrongdoing, we are then faced with another decision. Will we choose to wallow in self-punishment by beating ourselves over the head with more guilt, or will we choose to experience constructive sorrow? Our options look like this:

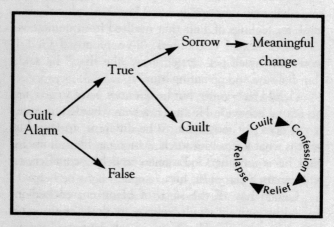

If you are in guilt's grip, choose the road less traveled—constructive sorrow and personal change. Follow these steps, and they will lead you on the way to godly sorrow:

1. Be honest.

When guilt is real, there is no escape. You may run, but there is no place to hide. To rid yourself of real guilt, you must start by taking responsibility for your misdeeds. You must be honest about the hurt you have caused others as well as the pain you have caused yourself.

2. Focus on the person who has been wronged.

Look beyond your own pain to see if others are also hurting. Make a list of persons you have harmed or hurt. In Gerald's case, he had violated a relationship with his date and had broken a promise with God. All he can see, however, is his own pain. By lifting his vision beyond his self-centered feelings, he could take steps to repair the damage and promote genuine healing.

3. Confess your misdeed.

The very act of confession is a healing process. Sometimes, however, confession can be used as an excuse to wallow in guilt. Therefore, confession must be done with discretion. When your confession is likely to cause more pain than healing, confess to an objective person who knows how to keep a confidence. A pastor or a therapist, for example, might be helpful. In Gerald's case, he chose to confess to a counselor. But regardless of how you confess and talk about your guilt to another person, it is critical that you confess your misdeed to yourself and to God.

4. Ask for forgiveness.

Fulton Sheen, a popular Catholic priest in the fifties and sixties, said, "The only unforgivable sin is the denial of sin, because by its very nature, there is now nothing to be forgiven." If possible, and without causing further damage, ask forgiveness from whomever you have wronged. It may be a friend, a family member, or a coworker. It may be God, or even yourself. Regardless of who it is, you must ask forgiveness for what you have done wrong. Gerald, for example, needed to ask the woman he had wronged to forgive him.

5. Make it right.

Restitution is an old-fashioned word, almost as unpopular as sin. According to the dictionary, restitution is "an act of restoring something to its rightful owner." In simpler days, stealing was usually related to tangibles such as hand tools or chickens. Restitution was fairly straightforward. Things are different now. Life is complicated with divorce settlements, faceless corporations, legal departments, accounting procedures, white collar crime, and so on. Restitution is sometimes a matter for the courts. Although restitution may be complicated, it is an important step in finding freedom from real guilt. In Gerald's case, he could not do much to repair the harm he had done other than to ask for forgiveness from his date.

6. Accept forgiveness.

Accepting forgiveness is often the most difficult step in healing guilt. The conscience doesn't want to give up its power. But you will not rid yourself of guilt until you take the final step of accepting forgiveness. Sometimes restitution is not possible. Sometimes the offended person refuses to forgive you. But that is her problem, not yours. If you are genuinely sorry, have honestly tried to make it right, and have sincerely asked God for forgiveness, you can be confident you are forgiven. "If we confess our sins, he is faithful and just to forgive us our sins" (1 John 1:9). Because Gerald had a difficult time accepting God's forgiveness, his self-condemnation kept him mired in his sin. By accepting forgiveness, he could be free of the guilt that would drive him to sin again.

7. Look to the future.

Asked which of his works was his masterpiece, architect Frank Lloyd Wright, at the age of eighty-three, replied, "My next one." Envision, in detail, the design of a better future rather than mulling over your past failures. Gerald was so consumed with how "rotten" he was for what he had done, he hadn't taken the time to construct a future that looked any different from his past.

8. Ask yourself why you want to change your behavior or attitude.

Do you want to promote growth and improve your relationships, or do you merely want to avoid the painful feelings of guilt? Gerald didn't really want to behave differently. He simply wanted to feel better about himself without having to sacrifice his selfish desires.

9. Rely on God's strength to help you overcome.

Humbly admit you are powerless to overcome your guilt alone, and make a decision to turn your will and life over to the care of God. Gerald, for example, was trying to be the kind of person he wanted to be without

depending on God's grace to help him change.
Therefore, he repeatedly fell into the same sin.

10. Respect who you are as a person.

You can be deeply remorseful without surrendering
your self-respect or dignity. Paul, who was "sorrowful,
yet always rejoicing," understood this (2 Cor. 6:10).
Gerald admitted his wrongdoing but did so in defeat.
In a state of helplessness, he was frustrated and angry
with himself. In this scenario, there was no place for
change.

In this chapter we have looked at how to handle
true guilt feelings effectively so as to diminish their
pain and make real and lasting changes in our lives. In
the next chapter we will examine the problem of false
guilt, which can be as debilitating as real guilt, but
whose cure requires a different approach.

6

Overcoming False Guilt

Knowing that her nine-year-old daughter, Nicole, was getting out of school at noon, Janice took a day off to run errands and spend time with Nicole. All morning she ran from place to place, shopping for groceries, picking up clothes at the dry cleaners, and depositing money at the bank. By noon she was home to greet Nicole and fix lunch. Then she and Nicole spent several hours baking a cake and planting bulbs in the garden. By 3:00 Janice was exhausted. She stretched out on the couch, intending to relax only for a moment, but she quickly fell asleep. When she woke fifteen minutes later, she found her daughter watching television. Janice kicked herself. "Here I was going to make this a special day for Nicole, and I have to go and fall asleep! I'm a terrible mother," she thought.

Janice, however, is *not* a terrible mother. She *had* fulfilled her intention of spending time with her daughter, and she obviously had needed a brief nap.

71

But Janice, because of her overactive conscience, struggles with the problem of false guilt.

In the previous chapter I showed how to deal with *real* guilt through the pathway of godly sorrow. But what do we do with *false* guilt? Since false guilt is not caused by any real wrongdoing, godly sorrow does not eradicate it. In fact, false guilt does not deserve the same treatment as true guilt. To apply God's forgiveness to guilt that does not exist cheapens his gift of grace. We must therefore be careful to distinguish between real and false guilt and apply the remedy that best treats the sickness.

Although there are no fail-safe remedies for the disease of false guilt, there are six steps you can take to ameliorate its pain and reduce the frequency of its attacks on your conscience.

1. Distinguish between real guilt and false guilt.

To review, real guilt is caused when we break the law—either the law of the land, or God's moral law. False guilt, however, is not a result of breaking any laws. Rather, false guilt is a trap and a lie devised by Satan to keep us in bondage to negative feelings.

At the root of false guilt is the idea that what you *feel* must be true—or, in other words, if you *feel* guilty, you think you must have *done* something wrong. However, emotions can lie, because they are not products of reality, but of our *interpretation* of reality. Distorted thoughts and beliefs give birth to emotional distortions.

If your guilt alarm won't stop sounding, ask yourself what objective evidence could be summoned to prove your fault. If you cannot find evidence of wrongdoing, you are suffering from false guilt, an emotion that is based on feeling, not fact.

2. Beware of expectations.

People suffer needless guilt when they put themselves at the mercy of their own expectations. In a sense, they are setting themselves up to fail by expecting more than they can possibly receive. Therefore, challenge your unspoken expectations in specific terms. For example, what do you expect at work? Do you think, "My boss will always recognize my good work and thank me for it"? What are your expectations at home? Do you ever think, "My family will praise me for how tidy the house is" or "They will recognize how hard I work to keep this home running on a predictable schedule"? What do you expect from your friends? Do you expect them never to let you down? What are your expectations about church? Do you expect everyone to be consistently loving and accepting?

Even posing these questions suggests their absurdity. Turn your expectations into wishes and even then, don't take them too seriously. If you want a little recognition for your hard work, then ask for it. Don't set yourself up to feel like a failure because someone hasn't responded in the way you deserve. Examine carefully your unrealistic expectations, for if they are unspoken they may also be unrecognized.

Take a moment to write down the private expectations that unwittingly set you up for battles with false guilt. This simple exercise will help you re-educate your conscience so you can become more flexible with yourself.

3. Say good-bye to perfectionism and hello to being human.

When a person wants to comfort a friend who has made a mistake, he'll often say, "You're only human—you're supposed to make mistakes!" Guilt-prone people, however, think they should never make any mistakes. They have unrealistic goals, and they ignore human weakness.

Perfection is the ultimate illusion, for it simply does not exist on this earth. When people try to live under self-imposed perfectionist standards, they will forever be tormented by unnecessary guilt. Their guilt will make them feel inept, disappointed, and depressed. One of my students, for example, felt he brought disgrace to his family by not making all A's. That is unreasonable. No one can be perfect!

Of course, this does not mean we should not aim for high standards. There is a difference between perfectionism and excellence. Thomas Peters and Robert Waterman, Jr., authors of the best-selling *In Search of Excellence*, describe excellence not as attaining an impossibly out-of-reach goal but as living up to your potential. Everyone, no matter how lowly, has the potential to attain excellence in his or her life.

When you wake up each morning, give yourself permission to be wrong! Strive for excellence, but not perfection. And as a human, remember you're *supposed* to make mistakes.

4. Realize it is okay to say no.

Are you able to say no to things you don't want to do and not feel guilty? Saying no to a request is not a sin. Some people believe that passive agreeableness is the same thing as virtue, decency, and honor. It is not. Passivity has more in common with wimpishness than civility or good manners.

I have always had difficulty saying no to speaking invitations. Some time ago my "yeses" were doled out so easily that my speaking schedule began to interfere with other important responsibilities. One day a kind and trusted colleague took me to lunch. He asked me about my speaking schedule and after patiently listening said, "Les, you know it's okay to say no, don't you?" Somehow his words helped me to set better boundaries, and I began to learn to meet other people's needs without sacrificing my own.

Do you also have difficulty saying no? Be honest. Ask yourself what you would do in these circumstances: A close friend asks you for a loan. Your least favorite aunt tells you she is coming to visit. A salesperson pressures you to buy his product. Your boss asks you to postpone your vacation. Your pastor asks you to teach the junior-high Sunday school class for the next eight weeks.

It is okay to disagree and it is okay to say no. If you are having difficulty standing your ground because guilt urges you to give in, learn to be assertive. To start with, ask for more time before making a decision. Give yourself an opportunity to think about the implications of "a small favor" before you agree to do it.

Next, ask yourself, "What am I feeling?" The guilt-prone person is more likely to ask, "What *should* I be feeling?" But this question is irrelevant. Focus on how you *honestly* feel. Once you have identified your feelings, talk about them with a trusted friend and get his or her objective feedback. Your feelings are neither good nor bad; they are just your feelings. Talking them out will clarify your thinking and help you reach a healthy decision. If you decide it is better to say no to a pushy salesperson or an intrusive relative, say no! A no doesn't even require an explanation. You don't have to feel guilty for setting up boundaries to protect your own sense of well-being.

5. Concentrate on being rather than doing.

Trying to *look* good is exhausting. It is less work and much more rewarding to focus instead on trying to *be* good. If false guilt is a hound at your heels, shift your focus from *doing* the right thing to *being* the right person.

God does not wait for us to do the right thing to accept us. In fact, Paul wrote, "But God demonstrates his own love for us in this: *While we were still sinners,* Christ died for us" (Rom. 5:8, emphasis mine). God's love and acceptance of us is what enables us to love and be kind to others: "We love because he first loved us" (1 John 4:19).

Think of what you are like when you are with a close circle of friends who accept you in spite of your blemishes. You are probably relaxed, happy, and loving. Now think what you are like around a group that withholds their acceptance of you until you have measured up to their expectations. Hoping to do and say the right things, you probably walk around on eggshells.

When we focus on *doing* rather than *being*, we more than double our chances of suffering from false guilt.

6. If you are still stuck, get help.

One of my favorite comics is a drawing of a boy in distress yelling to his dog: "Lassie, get help!" In the next frame, Lassie is lying on a couch in a psychologist's office.

If you have battled false guilt with little success, seek professional help. Once you speak about your struggles to someone you trust, relief is not far away. You will be able to view yourself from a freer, less tyrannical perspective. Putting your false guilt into words is the first step in battling love's unseen enemy—guilt.

Part Two

⁓

UNMASKING LOVE'S COUNTERFEITS

7

Identifying Your Relational Style: A Self-Test

Each of us has a certain way of relating to other people. Your relational style is an aspect of your personality and affects how you get along with your spouse, children, friends, and coworkers, and it even influences your relationship with God.

The following test will help you to identify your relational style. To keep your results accurate and unbiased, stop and take the test before reading any further. I will explain your test results later in the chapter.

THE TRAIT TEST

On the next page are a number of pairs of personal characteristics or traits. For each pair, choose the trait that you value more. Mark Ⓐ if you value being "imaginative," or Ⓑ if you value being "rational." Some of the traits will appear twice, but always in combination with a different trait. No pairs will be repeated.[1]

I would rather be . . .

Ⓐ	Ⓑ	
Ⓐ	Ⓑ	1. imaginative—rational
Ⓐ	Ⓑ	2. helpful—quick-witted
Ⓐ	Ⓑ	3. neat—sympathetic
Ⓐ	Ⓑ	4. level-headed—efficient
Ⓐ	Ⓑ	5. intelligent—considerate
Ⓐ	Ⓑ	6. self-reliant—ambitious
Ⓐ	Ⓑ	7. respectful—original
Ⓐ	Ⓑ	8. creative—sensible
Ⓐ	Ⓑ	9. generous—individualistic
Ⓐ	Ⓑ	10. responsible—original
Ⓐ	Ⓑ	11. capable—tolerant
Ⓐ	Ⓑ	12. trustworthy—wise
Ⓐ	Ⓑ	13. neat—logical
Ⓐ	Ⓑ	14. forgiving—gentle
Ⓐ	Ⓑ	15. efficient—respectful
Ⓐ	Ⓑ	16. practical—self-confident
Ⓐ	Ⓑ	17. capable—independent
Ⓐ	Ⓑ	18. alert—cooperative
Ⓐ	Ⓑ	19. imaginative—helpful
Ⓐ	Ⓑ	20. realistic—moral
Ⓐ	Ⓑ	21. considerate—wise
Ⓐ	Ⓑ	22. sympathetic—individualistic
Ⓐ	Ⓑ	23. ambitious—patient
Ⓐ	Ⓑ	24. reasonable—quick-witted

Now take a moment to score your test. Give yourself a point for each answer that matches the following key. Note that items 1, 4, 6, 8, 10, 13, 16, 17, and 24 are "buffer" items and are not used in the scoring.

2. a _____
3. b _____

    5. b _____
    7. a _____
    9. a _____
    11. b _____
    12. a _____
    14. a _____
    15. b _____
    18. b _____
    19. a _____
    20. b _____
    21. a _____
    22. a _____
    23. b _____
    Total: _____

Put the test aside for the moment. We will explore the significance of your score later in the chapter.

WHAT THE TEST MEASURES

The test you just took measures how much you value what are considered "loving" traits. To discover the influence of guilt on relationships, I gave this test and the guilt test from Chapter 1 to more than 1000 people across the country. I gave both tests because I was interested in how the emotion of guilt affects our ability to love.

Before I gave these tests, I predicted that if a person scored high on guilt he or she would score low on love. In other words, I predicted that a guilt-prone person would have a diminished capacity for loving other people. But my findings showed just the opposite: a great number of people scored high on both love *and* guilt. At this point it looked like guilt made people better lovers!

As I analyzed my findings, however, I realized that the love of the guilt-prone people lacked a critical component: the capacity for empathy.

WHAT IS EMPATHY?

Empathy is at the heart of love. It is the rare capacity to put ourselves into the shoes of another person and accurately see life from her perspective, then use that knowledge to meet her needs.

Empathy combines two important capacities: the capacity to analyze and the capacity to sympathize. Let's look at each of these capacities.

The Capacity to Analyze

Our analytical capacities involve our ability to *think*. We look at a problem like inner-city crime and break it down into its causes and propose solutions. We look at the problem rationally. We collect facts about it, observe its conditions, and look for ways to solve the problems. Analysis comes from the head and is based on facts.

The Capacity to Sympathize

Our sympathetic capacities involve our ability to *feel*. Many of us sympathize with those who are suffering. Our hearts ache when we see a picture of a starving child, or when we view another body being carried from the war-torn streets of inner-city Washington, D.C. When we sympathize with people, we feel for them. If they are suffering, we feel their pain. If they are angry, we feel their rage. Sympathy comes from the heart and is based on feelings.

Analysis + Sympathy = Empathy

While both analysis and sympathy are important, *neither one by itself can solve relationship problems.* Rather, we need to both analyze *and* sympathize—to use both our heads *and* our hearts—to address the complicated problems of human relationships. I call this combination of head and heart the capacity to empathize.

When we are empathetic, we use our imagination to put ourselves into other people's shoes and understand them. Putting aside our own needs and concerns, we focus on other people, and we ask ourselves questions like "What are they feeling? Why are they feeling that way? What pressures do they have to cope with? What do they fear? What do they need? How, if at all, should I help them?"

Empathy is an important skill in many professions. The best doctors are those who are not only highly trained, but also empathetic to your wishes and needs. The best counselors are able to "get inside your head" and understand what makes you tick. The best managers will look for what motivates you and makes you productive, then provide those things.

Empathy is crucial to family relationships. If you empathize with your tired, crying four-year-old, you will realize that he needs some quiet time, and you will cuddle and rock him instead of yelling at him to shut up. If you empathize with your wife, you will know what makes her feel loved and do it, whether that be writing her funny notes, giving her a daily back rub, or sending her flowers on special occasions. If you empathize with your teenage son, you will know the pressures he faces in school and give him the support he needs to combat those pressures.

True empathy involves risk. When you seek to understand another person by entering her world, you may find that you yourself need to change. Instead of condemning someone who struggles with alcoholism, you might offer to pray for his healing and support him as he goes through recovery. Instead of insulating yourself in a safe suburb and complaining about the rising crime rate, you might get involved with a mentorship program for inner-city teens, or you might help to renovate homes for the poor.

The best model of empathy was our Lord himself. If Jesus Christ had been merely sympathetic to our plight, he would have watched our struggles from afar, shaking his head and feeling bad. If he had been merely analytical, he would have told us exactly what to do, stripping us of our freedom and solving all our problems for us. Instead, the Son of God chose to become one of us.

The best summary of empathy can be found in Philippians 2:

> Do nothing out of selfish ambition or vain conceit, but in humility consider others better than yourselves. Each of you should look

not only to your own interests, but also to the interests of others. Your attitude should be the same as that of Christ Jesus: Who, being in very nature God, did not consider equality with God something to be grasped, but made himself nothing, taking the very nature of a servant, being made in human likeness. And being found in appearance as a man, he humbled himself and became obedient to death—even death on a cross! (Phil. 2:3–8)

But the story doesn't end there . . .

Therefore God exalted him to the highest place and gave him the name that is above every name, that at the name of Jesus every knee should bow, in heaven and on earth and under the earth, and every tongue confess that Jesus Christ is Lord, to the glory of God the Father. (Phil. 2:9–11)

Using Jesus as our model, we are called to "work out [our] salvation with fear and trembling" (Phil. 2:12). Empathy is not easy. It is *work*—such hard work that when Jesus faced his own death he sweat drops of blood at the Garden of Gethsemane. It is such hard work that sometimes we will want to run away from it. But the rewards of empathy are far greater than we can possibly imagine.

Obviously, few of us are able to be truly empathetic all the time. Instead, we tend to fall into certain patterns of behavior that seem to work best for us. Those patterns of relating seem to protect us from emotional pain, but in reality they isolate us from each other and prevent us from developing into whole, loving, mature people of God.

Let's look at those behaviors now.

FOUR RELATIONAL STYLES

From my research on love and guilt, I developed a model that describes four relational styles or patterns. Some people analyze but do not sympathize. I call these people *Controllers*. Other people sympathize but do not analyze. I call these people *Pleasers*. A third group neither analyzes or sympathizes. I call these people *Withholders*. Finally, some people are able to combine both analysis and sympathy; they empathize. I call these people *Lovers*.

Here is another way to look at these four relational styles. When I gave the two tests—one which tested for guilt and one which tested for love—I found that some people scored high on guilt, while others scored low. In addition, some people scored high on love, while others scored low. By combining their dispositions, these four groups emerged:

1. Pleasers, who are high on guilt and high on love.

2. Controllers, who are low on guilt and low on love.

3. Withholders, who are high on guilt and low on love.

4. Lovers, who are low on guilt and high on love.

	LOVE	
	High	Low

	High	**PLEASER**	**WITHHOLDER**
GUILT	Low	**LOVER**	**CONTROLLER**

The Pleaser

Pleasers tend to wallow in their feelings of guilt. They value loving traits, but they have difficulty empathizing. The Pleaser tends to sympathize, but not analyze. Pleasers "love" with their hearts, but not with their heads.

Pleasers are concerned with doing things right, but not necessarily with doing the right things. They love in order to feel good about themselves. In other words, they do loving things in order to relieve their guilt.

Pleasers are generally known to be sacrificial because they continually do things for other people. However, their so-called "helpful" deeds don't always meet the other person's needs. Their feelings are in the right place, but they lack the common sense and analytical capabilities to channel them in the right direction. So most of the time, Pleasers only meet needs by accident.

The Controller

These rugged individualists don't suffer from guilt, and they often find other things more important than love. Controllers are the mirror image of Pleasers. They analyze, but they don't sympathize. They "love" with their head but not with their heart.

Controllers can identify the problems and needs of others in an intellectual way, but they don't always exude warmth and concern. They emphasize rationality and see almost any form of sentimentality as a weakness. Controllers are goal oriented and are easily frustrated when things do not go as planned.

In relationships, Controllers are in obvious command. They are experts at getting their own needs met (especially from Pleasers) and sometimes turn critical. Their motto is: "If you want it done right, do it yourself."

The Withholder

Withholders, like Pleasers, carry a great deal of guilt, but they value other qualities more than love. Withholders rarely tap into their ability to empathize. The Withholder, in fact, will hardly sympathize.

Withholders fear rejection. They live in an anxious and egocentric world. It's not that they are selfish, just self-focused. They personalize their environment; in other words, they act as if everything that goes wrong is their own fault. They repress tenderness, and feelings of any kind are frightening.

Withholders, more likely than not, are survivors. They have been burned by past relationships, and some have even suffered abuse. Withholders have a Ph.D. in pain and are slow to risk experiencing the possible heartache of a new relationship.

The Lover

Lovers are free from guilt's grip and value love highly. Unlike Pleasers, Withholders, or Controllers, Lovers tap into their capacity for genuine empathy. Only Lovers are able both to analyze and sympathize, loving with their heads as well as their hearts.

Lovers are not thrown off balance by great surges of emotion, and neither do they work to shed feelings of guilt. Lovers strive to *be* loving, not simply *do* loving things. Unlike Controllers, Lovers do not build relationships for personal advantage. And unlike Pleasers, Lovers set boundaries to protect their personhood.

Lovers find fulfillment in the process of learning to love. They value personal growth, and they don't try to achieve a static condition of love that can be observed, approved, and applauded.

A Model

On the following page is a helpful diagram of the four groups:

| | **LOVE** | |
	High	Low
High	**PLEASER** *Sympathizes*	**WITHHOLDER** *Personalizes*
Low	**LOVER** *Empathizes*	**CONTROLLER** *Analyzes*

(Left vertical axis labeled: **GUILT**, *with* High *at top and* Low *at bottom.)*

To quickly summarize these styles, the Pleaser says, "I'm not okay, but you're okay." The Withholder says, "I'm not okay, and you're not okay, and I'll point that out to you if you get too close." The Controller says, "I'm okay, and you might be okay if you do what I want you to do." And the Lover says, "I'm not okay, and you're not okay, but isn't that okay?"

WHAT'S YOUR STYLE?

By this time, I am sure you are eager to make sense of your own test scores and discover what relational style you tend to employ.

Turn back to the the Trait Test you took at the beginning of this chapter and look at your total. As I mentioned, this test reveals how much you value loving traits. There are fifteen possible points on the Trait Test. If you scored seven points or more, you are probably in the "high love" zone. Below seven points puts you in the "low love" zone.

In Chapter 1 you measured how guilt-prone you tend to be. If you scored above a forty on this test, you are probably in the "high guilt" zone. Below thirty-nine points puts you in the "low guilt" zone. The scoring looks like this:

	Trait Test	Guilt Test
Pleasers	7 or more	40 or more
Withholders	6 or less	40 or more
Controllers	6 or less	39 or less
Lovers	7 or more	39 or less

Now a word of caution. No one can be reduced to a few numbers and labeled. Whatever "your quadrant," you are not neatly contained by its parameters. We all swim in and out of these boundaries daily. If you are primarily a Controller, for example, there will be times when you are more like a Pleaser or a Withholder. During some sterling moments you will enter the camp of the Lover. But if you scored deep within a certain zone, you will tend to operate most naturally from that position.

The point of these tests is not to put you in a box but to help you identify and fix what may be quietly undermining your relationships. As you learn more about these behaviors, you will discover how to become more loving, using both your head and your heart to empathize with the people around you.

CULTIVATING THE SOIL FOR HEALTHY RELATIONSHIPS

Long before I discovered these four relational styles, Jesus identified them in the parable of the sower (Matt. 13:1–23). Although Jesus used the types of soil to describe how people would respond to his words, the categories can also be used to describe the four relational styles discussed in this book.

Some soil that Jesus described was hard, and the seed never took root. Instead, birds came and snatched up the seed (Matt. 13:4). This rejecting soil is like the Withholder, who refuses to cultivate the seeds of loving relationships.

Some soil was shallow. The seed took root and sprang up quickly, but soon it died under the consuming sun (Matt. 13:5). This soil evokes Pleasers, who are quick to help but soon burn out. Their shallow, sympathizing style prevents authentic love from taking root.

Other seeds fell on thorny soil, where cultivation was impossible (Matt. 13:7). This soil is like the Controller's analytical style, which resists the feelings of spontaneity and enthusiasm and nurtures the weeds that stifle growth.

Finally, there was the good soil, which was free from the pests of guilt (Matt. 13:8). Seeds of love sown in this soil produce a bountiful harvest of loving relationships.

In the next four chapters you will become better acquainted with the ways of the Pleaser, the Controller, and the Withholder. But most of all, I invite you to learn the ways of the Lover.

8

Compulsive Love: The Pleaser

"If I don't help her, who will?" The question hung between us like a wisp of smoke. "I mean, if I were in her shoes . . . " Jenny's voice broke, and she gave way to tears.

Jenny is thirty-eight; her husband, David, had made the appointment for them to see me. Looking at Jenny anxiously, he said, "Doc, I'm afraid she is going to have a nervous breakdown. Ever since her mother moved into that retirement center Jen hasn't been the same. She goes to Little League games with our son, she coordinates the nursery program at church, she informally counsels countless women, and now she is taking care of her bedridden mother in a center that is designed to do that for her."

David paused and looked at his wife. "Jen, you can't say no! You've always taken on too much, but now that your mother is close by, it has put you over the edge."

Still wiping at her eyes, Jenny said, "I know I'm doing an awful lot, but it's just—"

"—Don't say it's just for a short time," David

interrupted. "You've been doing this for more than five months, and it's taking its toll. You can hardly sleep. You have no time for me. Even your mother says stop! Enough is enough."

Jenny is suffering from what I call "compulsive love." She is engulfed in an overwhelming sense of responsibility and has an almost bottomless well of desire to help. Guilt lurks in the shadows of her mind. She is troubled not by the wrong she has done, but by the good she feels she has left undone. Jenny is trying to help all the people around her, but she is hurting the people closest to her by spreading herself too thin.

Jenny's heart is as big as a mountain, but she doesn't realize that loving too much has kept her from giving to the ones she loves what they need. She has confused "doing for" with "caring about." Jenny is trying to prove to herself how much she loves her mother and everyone else, instead of figuring out what would really be best for them.

Jenny, like thousands of others, is a Pleaser.

	High	**LOVE**	Low
High	**PLEASER** *Sympathizes*		**WITHHOLDER** *Personalizes*
Low	**LOVER** *Empathizes*		**CONTROLLER** *Analyzes*

GUILT

The Pleaser's Profile: Pleasers place a high value on acts of love, but their loving is frustrated by equally strong feelings of guilt. Pleasers respond out of emotion. They sympathize but don't analyze. They love with their hearts but not with their heads.

WHO IS THE PLEASER?

In the early days of aviation, pilots used a descriptive phrase, "Flying by the seat of your pants." Before instruments for aerial navigation were available, the only guide was the pilot's own sense of movement. If he felt pressure on the seat of his aircraft, it probably meant he was ascending, much the same as the feeling you get in a rising elevator. Conversely, if he felt weightless, the plane was probably descending. This means of flying, of course, was not at all reliable. Men died because their feelings played tricks on their judgment.

Feelings can be just as deadly when they are used to navigate relationships, although Pleasers are often blind to the danger. Pleasers tend to rely solely on their emotions to tell them what to do and how to respond. And since feelings of guilt tug the Pleaser like strings on a puppet, Pleasers are often motivated to do the "right things" for the wrong reasons.

Pleasers march to the beat of somebody else's drum. They have a compliant personality and try desperately to make others happy. As children, their primary goal was not to get all A's or to be a cheerleader or president of the class. Instead, they strived to be popular or to make their parents happy.

The classic biblical Pleaser was Jesus' friend,

Martha. They first met when Martha opened her home to Jesus and his disciples. Martha scurried about making preparations to serve the men, while her sister, Mary, simply sat and listened to Jesus. Finally, Martha complained, "Lord, don't you care that my sister has left me to do the work by myself? Tell her to help me!"

"Martha, Martha," Jesus answered. "You are worried and upset about many things, but only one thing is needed. Mary has chosen what is better, and it will not be taken away from her" (Luke 10:40–42).

Martha was more concerned with *doing* loving things than *being* a loving person. She was attending to everyone else's needs, but she did not recognize her own need to sit at the feet of Jesus. Only later, when her faith in Jesus had grown, was she able to put aside her own worries and trust him even in the worst of circumstances—when her beloved brother, Lazarus, had died.

You may be a **PLEASER** if . . .

- you sense a strong urge to make others happy, even at the expense of your own happiness.
- you enjoy giving, but receiving makes you feel indebted.
- you routinely wonder what others think of how you act.
- you carry a sense of responsibility for things beyond your control.
- you stuff you personal needs and desires.
- you cringe at the possibility of having to confront someone.

My research revealed that the majority of Pleasers are women. This is no surprise. Women are trained socially to nurture and please others. Even today, when women can crew space capsules and run for political office, many of them still feel guilty when they are not totally selfless in their personal lives. Guilt afflicts the stay-at-home mother, who worries about family finances; the working woman, who worries about child care; and the single mother, who worries about her child's lack of a father.

Women, however, by no means have a monopoly on guilt. Men also suffer from self-inflicted guilt. Some men, for example, find themselves pursuing career advancement, not for personal fulfillment, but to please their spouses. Some helpaholic men can't say no and commit themselves to innumerable good causes. Some husbands, fueled by guilt, take it upon themselves to shield their families from the normal wear-and-tear of daily living. While there is no shortage of male Pleasers, however, more often than not, the Pleaser is a woman.

THE PLEASER'S SYMPATHETIC STYLE

Sympathy is derived from a Greek term meaning "with feeling." And Pleasers are expert feelers, experiencing the depths of pain, agony, suffering, distress, anguish, grief, and compassion. But their feelings often cause them to jump to unfounded conclusions, which are based more on feelings than facts. Pleasers unwittingly project their own neediness onto others and then meet those "needs" as a way of meeting their own.

Consider Jenny from the beginning of this chapter. She was so busy trying to feel less guilty about her mother's bedridden condition that she tried to meet needs her mother did not have. For example, she would sit at her mother's side idly thumbing through magazines while her mother napped—just to be there when her mother's eyes opened. To Jenny this was a loving gesture. Her mother, however, didn't *want* Jenny to visit while she was sleeping! She would have preferred to see Jenny when she was rested and ready to receive visitors. But Jenny's motivation to visit her mother was governed by her own nagging conscience, not by the desires of her mother.

Doing "loving" things helps Pleasers feel better about themselves and perhaps assuages a bit of their guilt in the process. But "loving" behavior that is not grounded in empathy is not always helpful—and sometimes, as in Jenny's case, it does more harm than good.

Pleasers, even those with good intentions, are handicapped because they lack the capacity to empathize. Empathy is the only door for entering another person's world and meeting his or her deepest needs. Because the secrets of the heart are closed to anyone who comes calling without empathy, Pleasers are often left out in the cold, and they never find the intimacy that they are working so hard to achieve.

THE PLEASER'S RELATIONSHIPS

Numerous studies, including my own, confirm that the emotion of guilt quietly sabotages relationships.

This fact becomes painfully clear in the life of the Pleaser. While Pleasers yearn for strong, healthy relationships, their relationships are built on the shaky foundation of self-condemnation and guilt.

Pleasers' relationships are characterized by: (1) the need to please, (2) giving, not receiving, (3) a performance mentality, (4) overresponsibility, (5) self-denial as an end instead of a means, (6) avoidance of conflict, and (7) a deferring style of communication.

The Need to Please

This need, of course, is the foundation of all Pleasers' relationships. And this need to please makes them easy to be around. After all, Pleasers are terrified by the slightest possibility of snubbing someone or hurting someone's feelings. Pleasers are the ones others turn to when they need a nonthreatening shoulder to cry on.

Pleasers have an easy smile. They are approachable and always agreeable. Pleasers have found the "secret" for instant affection: people like people who have the good sense to like them and show their appreciation. They have made this approach second nature and are skilled at winning approval.

Pleasers, however, have taken a good thing too far. They are frenetically trying to make everyone happy, but the harder they try, the more they fail. As Pulitzer prize–winning journalist Henry Bayard Swope noted: "I cannot give you the formula for success, but I can give you the formula for failure: Try to please everybody."

Giving, Not Receiving

I spoke to a group of homeless people at a mission in downtown Seattle some years ago. After my brief talk, the director of the mission stood up to close the meeting. "Before we are dismissed," he said, "I want to invite you to participate in an offering to show our appreciation for Dr. Parrott's words."

I was shocked and embarrassed. I tried to pull at his sleeve from behind the podium and tell him not to do that. He brushed my hand away. Before I left the mission that night, he handed me an envelope filled with loose coins and said, "To not accept their gift would be an insult." I humbly received their eighty-four cent gift and learned the lesson that giving is also receiving.

Pleasers submerge themselves in meeting the needs of others and almost always feel uneasy when they are on the receiving end. They see their only legitimate role in relationships as slaving to make others happy. When a gift is "forced" upon them, it adds to their debt of guilt and triggers a feverish compulsion to repay it.

We actually do a service when we are being served. Receiving from others is an act of humility and recognizes another's dignity and worth. Allowing others to serve us shows our respect and love for the server.

A Performance Mentality

The Pleaser is like the monk, Tanko, in an Anthony de Melo story. One rainy day, Tanko and another monk named Busho were traveling to another monastery when they came across a gigantic mud puddle. A young woman in a lovely kimono stood looking forlornly at the puddle, which blocked her way. Busho went up to her and said, "Would you like some help?" She nodded. "Well, then," Busho exclaimed, "jump up on my back." She did, and Busho waded across the road and gently put her down on the other side. Then he and Tanko continued their journey through the mud and rain.

Tanko and Busho arrived at their destination just before nightfall, tired and hungry. They washed and then were fed a good meal by the other monks. After dinner Tanko said, "Busho, how could you have carried that woman? You know that we monks are not supposed to have anything to do with women. Yet you invited one to actually jump on your back, and not only that, but a young and beautiful one. What might people have said if they had seen you? You disgraced your vows and our order. How could you?"

Busho looked at him. "Tanko, are you still carrying around that young woman?" he asked. "Why, I put her down over five hours ago!"[1]

The Pleaser is more concerned with doing things right than doing the right thing. They are more concerned with *looking* good than *being* good. Pleasers never enjoy a relationship for its own sake. Instead, they live secondhand from the compliments of others. Like a periscope scanning the sea, Pleasers are on the lookout for the approval that will ease their guilt. They have one eye on their action and the other on their audience.

Overresponsibility

The Pleaser suffers from "omnipotent guilt." This brand of guilt rests on the illusion of responsibility. A

Pleaser mother, for example, believes that she alone is responsible for her child's happiness and well-being. If her child sprains an ankle, she is to blame. And if she is out having fun when her child sprains the ankle, she feels twice as guilty.

Pleasers take on responsibility for more than they can possibly handle. They believe two lies: (1) "If I don't do it, it won't get done," and (2) "Everyone else's needs take priority over mine."[2]

Pleasers see someone in pain and assume responsibility for his healing. They have to right all wrongs, fill all needs, and soothe all hurts. Like Atlas, they carry the burdens of the world on their shoulders. Their overresponsibility, however, saps their strength until they are unable to be truly responsible for what falls squarely into their own lap.

Paradoxically, Pleasers take on an unreasonable amount of responsibility for things beyond their control but avoid responsibility for things they *can* do something about. The Pleaser, for instance, will stay up all night listening to a friend talk about her problems and give no thought to how staying up late will affect her work the next day. The Pleaser feels more responsible for solving her friend's problems than she feels for her own health or her ability to work.

Self-Denial as an End Instead of a Means

In his sermon "The Weight of Glory," C. S. Lewis warns of the dangers of being immoderately unselfish: "Unselfishness carries with it the suggestion not primarily of securing good things for others, but of going without them ourselves, as if our abstinence and not their happiness was the important point." Genuine love is not about doing without. Love may involve self-denial, but only as a means to meeting others' needs. The Pleaser, however, turns the means of self-denial into an end. And that's when "loving" behavior is no longer loving. We can give our bodies to be burned, as Scripture says, and still not be loving (1 Cor. 13:3).

The Pleaser "does unto others" whatever will make her look most loving. C. S. Lewis wrote an epitaph for a Pleaser whose self-sacrifice was an end instead of a means:

> Erected by her sorrowing brothers
> In memory of Martha Clay.
> Here lies one who lived for others.
> Now she has peace. And so have they.

Pleasers seem to feel that they have no right to do anything for their own sakes, and their martyr complex drives the people around them crazy.

Avoidance of Conflict

It has been said that people are like teabags—you never know how strong they are until they are in hot water. When Pleasers land in hot water, they immediately try to get out of it. They try to minimize conflict, and they always try to put the best face on things. They rarely air frustrations or ask difficult questions. Their ironclad rule is: Don't rock the boat.

Mahatma Gandhi said, "A 'No' uttered from deepest conviction is better and greater than a 'Yes' merely uttered to please, or what is worse, to avoid trouble."

Pleasers, unfortunately, are more likely to dole out yeses to avoid making waves. They rarely say, "My feelings got hurt when you . . . " or "I think we need to resolve this problem you and I are having." It is not the Pleaser's style to confront conflict head on. However, sooner or later Pleasers will be cornered and forced into conflict. At this point they either give in ("I'm to blame, it's my fault"), or they explode.

Even Pleasers have limits. Once their simmering unmet needs begin to boil, they turn into resentment. They teeter on the brink of anger, and if they fall, Pleasers almost always pull out their trump card: "After all I've done for you, I can't believe I have to put up with . . . " When the Pleaser explodes, it's like watching a kitten turn into a pit bull.

Deferring Style of Communication

Friend: "Where would you like to go for dinner?"

Pleaser: "Wherever."

Friend: "Well, I always choose. It's your turn."

Pleaser: "It really doesn't matter to me. Whatever you like is fine."

Friend: "C'mon, you've got to have an opinion about where you eat."

Pleaser: "I really don't. I like whatever you do."

This tiresome game of verbal ping-pong stretches on and on with Pleasers. They defer making decisions and giving their own opinions to everyone else. Because Pleasers value others more than themselves, they tend to have an "I-lose, you-win" communication pattern that is characterized by giving in, surrendering, and pretending.

Pleasers do a great deal of pretending. They pretend, for example, that they were not hurt as children. They pretend that their needs are being met. They pretend that they are not annoyed. They pretend that they do not feel powerless. And all their pretenses impact their communication.

Pleasers suffer from what experts call "communication apprehension." It is fueled by low self-esteem and a dreadful fear of not being socially accepted. So, in an attempt to appear acceptable, Pleasers defer to others. It helps them avoid the risk of responsibility ("What if he doesn't like the restaurant I choose?") and helps them feel more loving ("At least I was sensitive to his preferences").

The **PLEASER's** Strengths
- a willing heart
- contagious energy
- a keen ability to identify feelings
- a warm interpersonal style
- a team orientation
- a conscientious and caring attitude
- approachable and friendly
- action oriented

AN EIGHT-STEP PLAN FOR PLEASERS

If you are a Pleaser, scoring high on love and high on guilt, you know the drain of trying to build healthy relationships with only limited success. For most

Pleasers, being in a relationship is like holding the accelerator all the way down but keeping the car in neutral and a foot on the brake. Relationships consume your energies, but they take you nowhere fast.

The following steps are designed to help you build on your strengths and move you from sympathy to empathy, from loving with only your heart to loving with your head as well.

1. Admit your deficits.

Pleasers, like everyone else but even more so, have difficulty admitting they need help. After all, Pleasers are the ones trying to find their worth in giving, not receiving. But if you are to build healthy relationships that are mutually fulfilling, you must be honest with yourself and admit your deficits. Instead of hiding behind a general statement like "I am such a bad person," discover what your specific faults are, then work on correcting them.

Admit your error by tapping into your reason. Objectivity is the key. It may help to talk with a trusted friend, someone you respect, who will be honest and help you grow. Ask for objective feedback on your interpersonal style, and take to heart your friend's impressions.

2. Identify your own needs and desires.

Pleasers need to realize that shortchanging themselves also shortchanges their friends and family. Pleasers, if they do not identify their own needs and desires, eventually become martyrs. I know people who have chosen to play the role of martyr, or have arranged to have that role assigned to them in a family or work setting. They take all the pain and all the blame on themselves. They seem to have no wishes of their own, but merely substitute them with the wishes of others. Some are men or women whose spouses abuse them. Some are spouses of alcoholics or compulsive gamblers.

What would you like to do if you weren't caught up in taking care of everyone else? If you are like most Pleasers, you probably don't even know. In a desperate search for self-esteem, you have listened to others but never to yourself. You play an endless mental tape that says, "Everyone else's needs are more important than mine." But that is a lie. Your needs are critically important. If you do not identify your own needs, you can never accurately meet the needs of others.

Make a list of your personal needs and desires, things that do not depend on positive feedback from others. If you are a Pleaser, this exercise will be as much fun as petting snakes, but it is worth the effort. Write down anything that comes to mind. Putting your needs and desires on paper is part of acknowledging that they are real.

3. Practice self-assertion.

A recovering Pleaser once told me, "I used to feel terribly guilty when I asked for more iced tea or bread at a restaurant. Sometimes I still cringe when I have to speak up for my own needs." Most Pleasers would rather suffer in silence than make their needs known.

I have watched Pleasers collapse from fatigue, drown in depression, and develop debilitating illnesses because they did not assert themselves. Some doctors even call cancer "the disease of nice people." Surgeon

Bernie Siegel tells about one of his cancer patients who never expressed displeasure at anything. He said she began to improve, however, after she was able to tell her husband that she didn't like the family dog. He says, "People who always smile, never tell anyone their troubles, and neglect their own needs are the ones who are most likely to become ill. For them, the main problem often is learning to say no without guilt."[3]

Learn to make your needs known and practice getting them met by taking baby steps. Ask a friend for a small favor. Request something of your spouse. If you are leaving your house and the phone rings, let it ring. I once gave an assignment to a passive patient that required her to request a new spoon in a restaurant. It took five meals, but she did it! Assertiveness grows with each successful step.

4. *Face up to conflict.*

Pleasers operate from a book of etiquette that reads: "Don't do or say anything that might offend someone else. If someone does or says something that offends, annoys, or irritates you, act as if nothing has happened and pretend you are not bothered in the least."

Pleasers are so accustomed to being well-mannered they are able to deploy their good manners without even thinking about what they are doing. They unconsciously minimize and ignore conflict the way a cat avoids water.

"Where there is no difference," says Louis Nizer, "there is only indifference." If you are in a meaningful and caring relationship, you cannot avoid turbulence. Conflict is a part of life. It is not a sign of being unloving. Conflict, in fact, means you care and opens the way to healthier relationships. The rewards for facing up to conflicts and resolving them out in the open are great: peace of mind, increased trust, and deeper intimacy.

So don't run from disagreement. Don't sweep differences under the rug. Confront what offends, annoys, or irritates you. This does not mean lambasting someone you disagree with. It means acknowledging there is a problem and looking for a constructive way to solve that problem.

When you are trying to solve a conflict, begin by using "I-statements" to convey your thoughts. Never use "you-statements"—they sound accusatory and may cause an argument. For example, if you say, "I wanted to take a short walk with you after dinner instead of sitting down to watch TV" you are clearly stating your need and opening the problem to discussion. However, if you said, "You never want to take a walk, you just sit in front of that tube," you are sure to have a fight on your hands!

Pleasers always face relational friction with fear and dread. However, your uncomfortable feelings are a sign that you are moving closer to developing more loving relationships.

5. Acknowledge individual differences.

In a study of perception, researchers designed a split-screen viewing apparatus that could simultaneously flash two separate photos before one's eyes in a split second. For example, they showed at the same time a photo of a bullfighter and a photo of a baseball player. When they ran the experiment in Spain, the subjects almost always reported seeing a bullfighter. In America, subjects saw a baseball player.

We all look at the world through the lens of our personal experiences and values. We can't afford to assume that other people are interpreting their condition in the same way we would if we were in their shoes. We have to set our feelings in abeyance and objectively assess their world. We have to empathize.

We can't treat other people the way they want to be treated until we accurately understand what they want. Henry Ford said, "If there is any one secret of success, it lies in the ability to get the other person's point of view and see things from that person's angle as well as from your own."

Empathy allows you to understand that a friend who is going through a divorce may have different feelings about the situation than you would if you were him. Empathy helps you to recognize that celebrating a birthday may not hold the same meaning for someone else. Empathy forces you to realize that what seems desirable to you may be a turnoff for someone else.

Take time to analyze people's circumstances before you jump "heart-first" into helping them. Ask them about their experiences, and be careful not to hear what you want to hear in their response. Listen with sensitivity and objectivity, and avoid projecting your feelings onto them. This exercise will help turn your sympathy into empathy.

6. Focus on persons rather than your performance.

Something almost always goes wrong when we love others out of a desire to look like a loving person. French novelist François Mauriac tells a story called "The Woman of the Pharisees." In the story a wealthy woman visits the poor people in her village regularly and always leaves behind a gift. But before she leaves, the wealthy woman says, "You could improve your situation if you really worked at it."

This woman never left a poor family's house without making them feel worse for her having been there. She flogged them with kindness, and they hated her for her gifts. The woman was more concerned with looking like a loving person than she was with meeting the needs of hurting people.

Ask yourself how important your "loving image" is. Be honest. Do you strive to *look* loving rather than *be* loving? Who are you trying to impress and why? By becoming aware of your hidden motives, you can change them. Then, instead of using your energies to impress an audience, you will be using them to actually help people in need.

7. Beware of perpetual patterns of pleasing.

As I mentioned earlier, I work as a medical psychologist in the burn unit of a hospital. Before we discharge a burn patient, I always meet with the relatives, and I tell them not to do anything on the patient's first day home from the hospital that they don't want to do for the rest of their lives. I have seen too many families make "temporary" changes (like putting the patient's bed in the family room) that become permanent.

We all fall into unhealthy patterns without realizing it. Since you are prone to pleasing, watch out for situations that pull you into pleasing behaviors. Stop for a moment and think back on the people whom you have worked hardest to help. Look for patterns of pleasing that you commonly fall into. Make note of what triggers your urge to make others happy

and consider ways of keeping your urge to please
under control.

I worked with a Pleaser who routinely sacrificed
his Saturday afternoons to help people out with his
pickup truck. His family resented his rationalizations.
"It will only take me an hour or so to help this fella
move his desk," he would tell them. When his wife
confronted him with the actual number of weekends
he had spent helping others with his truck, he was
shocked. "I had no idea," he told me. "That's all it took
for me to set some limits and stick to them."

8. *Rid yourself of guilt and shame.*

In Chapters 5 and 6, I outlined the basic strategies
for resolving true guilt and false guilt. It is important to
remember that guilt and shame are at the root of the
Pleaser's problems. Don't attempt to break free from
pleasing until you have loosened guilt's grip. Practicing
these steps without first resolving your guilt would be
like a woodpecker trying to make a nest in a concrete
pole: your work will be fruitless, and you will probably
hurt yourself in the process!

9

Convenient Love: The Controller

Alan, age thirty-four and single, was dressed in a dark blue tailored suit and a crisply starched shirt. "This is the toughest thing I have ever done," he told me. "I have never been to a psychologist before, and I have always looked down on people who need a shrink."

Alan runs one of the swankiest restaurants in town. As he sat in a comfortable leather chair looking uncomfortable, I assured him he was not a "failure" for seeking psychotherapy. Then I said, "Tell me what brings you to see me."

"Every time I go into the kitchen at work," he confided, "I yell at the cooks because they are wasting too much food. I yell at the waitresses and the busboys for moving too slowly. If my people aren't living up to my standards, which is most of the time, I jump all over them."

"You've worked in the restaurant business for a long time?" I probed.

"I have grown up in it. My dad was a restaurant owner and my mom kept the books. I know what it takes to run this business and I kinda expect everyone else to know what I want them to do." Alan paused for a moment, and a wave of sadness flooded his serious face. "But it's killing me."

Alan went on to tell me that he recently learned from his doctor that his blood pressure was sky-rocketing and that he had to moderate his stressful lifestyle. He told me that he rarely takes a day off work because he likes to be a "hands-on" manager. He also told me that his social life leaves much to be desired. "I date women from time to time," he said, shrugging his shoulders, "but I'm usually too picky or they can't put up with my schedule."

Alan has a sharp mind and a quick wit. He is efficient, goal-oriented, factual, and logical. He is a problem solver who reaches conclusions step by reasonable step. Because he grew up in a home where most of his parents' love was enjoyed by his younger sister, he has repressed most of his warm and tender emotions. Alan learned to cope by stopping himself from needing or wanting love. He found his safety in being strong, tough, powerful, self-sufficient, and master of his own fate.

Alan has lived his whole life trying to maintain a position of "top dog." He has never admitted fear to anyone and is seen by some admirers as ambitious and aggressive. His enemies, however, see him as demanding and arrogant.

Alan, like thousands of others, is a Controller.

	High	LOVE	Low
High	**PLEASER** *Sympathizes*		**WITHHOLDER** *Personalizes*
GUILT			
Low	**LOVER** *Empathizes*		**CONTROLLER** *Analyzes*

The Controller's Profile: Controllers are not plagued with feelings of guilt and, relatively speaking, do not place a high value on loving traits. Controllers respond out of reason, not emotion. They analyze but don't sympathize. They love with their heads but seldom with their hearts.

WHO IS THE CONTROLLER?

Four college students decided they needed an extra day to cram for a Monday exam, so they devised a fail-proof scam. They left town for the weekend. When they returned on Tuesday, they went to see their professor. Producing dated receipts for a hotel and other expenses, they explained that their car got a flat tire, and they hadn't had a spare.

The professor agreed to give them a make-up exam in the form of a single written question. The students took their seats in separate corners of the exam room, silently crowing over their triumph—until the professor wrote the exam question on the blackboard: "Which tire?"

Controllers, like these students, find ways to work the system and get what they want without so much as a pinch from their conscience. But rarely are Controllers so blatantly caught in the act of "controlling" as they were by this professor. It sometimes takes one crafty Controller to recognize and stop another.

Controllers, in many ways, are the opposite of Pleasers. They tend to perceive sentimental emotions like tenderness, caring, and sympathy as "weak." They are more concerned with cleverness than kindness, with creativity than compassion, with self-confidence than self-sacrifice, with leadership than love.

The most heinous Controller in the Bible was King Herod. Not only did he kill every baby under two to protect his own throne from the threat of a superseding king, he even murdered his own wife and two sons because he thought they wanted him dead.

In his own humorous and bungling way, the disciple Peter, too, was a Controller. He kept trying to tell Jesus what to do and what to say, to the point where Jesus had to rebuke him sharply: "Get behind me, Satan! You are a stumbling block to me; you do not have in mind the things of God, but the things of men." Finally, humbled by his denial of Jesus, Peter became an effective leader of the new church, even admitting his fault when Paul confronted him for forcing Gentiles to follow Jewish laws (Gal. 2:11–14).

Controllers are very much like Pleasers once you crack their emotional code. Both are yearning for acceptance, but they travel different paths to find it. While the Pleaser yields power to others in an attempt to win their affection, the Controller takes charge to win their respect. Both are trying to earn love from others. And both fear rejection. The Pleaser believes rejection could come from offending, and the Controller believes it could come from failure.

You may be a **CONTROLLER** if . . .
- you dominate others in your relationships
- you are rarely moved by emotions
- you do not have difficulty getting your own needs met
- you blame, pressure, threaten, and criticize to get things done
- you are repulsed by sentimentalism
- you are hard to please

So Controllers live a lie that says: "If I am a success, people will love me." They are task-oriented, rugged individualists, striving for power, trying to be the best, the strongest, and the most capable. Death, illness, and economic change are all insults to their self-esteem, because they cannot control them.

Controllers dread anything that can weaken their status. To protect themselves from being vulnerable, Controllers deny their softer side and disengage their "weak" emotions. They are always on guard looking for attacks, but they also crave affirmations. Like the Pleaser they need the good opinion of others to bolster their sense of worth.

While there are women Controllers—Jezebel, Cleopatra, Evita, and Scarlett O'Hara are a few of the most famous—most Controllers are men. Just as women are socialized to please others, men are warned against being a sissy or a cry-baby. Men learn to suppress their emotions. The performance pressures that are typically placed on men and the expectation that they will rise above fear, pain, and self-doubt move males to use their heads more than their hearts.

In general Controllers are able to sort out the difference between an objective state of guilt and the feelings of subjective, self-imposed guilt. For this reason, they are rarely troubled by guilt feelings. Instead of punishing themselves with guilt pangs, Controllers have learned to escape their guilt through repression and projection. Their ability to repress guilt also gives Controllers the capacity to exploit the guilt feelings of others. This, in turn, gives them more influence and power.

Controllers harness their feelings of guilt and make them work for, not against, themselves. Controllers' repressed guilt becomes the high-octane fuel of ambition, driving them to achieve in an unconscious attempt to cleanse their souls. Unfortunately, this repression results in a hardening of the compassionate heart. Their guilt stands as a barrier to healthy, well-balanced relationships.

THE CONTROLLER'S ANALYTIC STYLE

The Controller's interpersonal style is a mirror image of the Pleaser's. While the Pleaser has sympathy but not objectivity, the Controller has objectivity but not sympathy. Unlike the Pleaser, the Controller can accurately understand others, but his emotions lag behind and keep intimacy and empathy out of reach. The Controller has a sluggish heart.

Charles F. Kettering said, "There is a great difference between knowing and understanding: you can know a lot about something and not really understand it." The Hebrew verb meaning "to know" is somewhat like the English word "understand." It can mean either to have information about someone or to be emotionally tied with someone. The Controller's "understanding" comes down on the side of having information. It misses out on the intimacy that understanding was designed to create.

Chaim Potok's novel *The Chosen* tells the story of a young boy born to a Hasidic rabbi. As the boy matures, his father recognizes that his child is especially clever and gifted, if not already a little arrogant and impatient. Knowing that his boy is likely to become the rabbi of his people, the father makes a mysterious and difficult decision not to speak to the boy. As the story draws to a close, Potok reveals that the father has chosen this unconventional way to raise his son because he wanted to create in him the capacity for understanding and compassion. He wanted his son to minister from a heart that knows pain and can feel the pain of others. The father feared that his son's analytic brilliance and arrogance would rob him of the capacity to empathize. The father in Potok's novel understood how keen analytic abilities, unsoftened by emotional tenderness, lead to manipulation rather than ministry.

While the Controller's analytic ability does empower him to understand the needs of others, this knowledge is often used to gain control over them rather than to meet their needs. Tom Sawyer, for example, was an expert Controller. He saw that his friends were bored and tricked them into doing his work—whitewashing a fence—for him!

THE CONTROLLER'S RELATIONSHIPS

The Controller's relationships are characterized by: (1) a need to be in control, (2) self-reliance, (3) an absence of emotion, (4) love as a means, not as an end, (5) rigid rules, (6) labeling, and (7) a demanding style of communication.

Need to Be in Control

Controllers are rugged individualists who want to take charge, and they typically use two powerful tools in gaining and maintaining control. The first is fear. Controllers have refined the technique of "winning through intimidation." They have a hawklike eye for weakness in others, and the people around them sense it. Without so much as a peep, the Controller fires fear and anxiety into others like Rambo fires a machine gun.

The second tool of control is guilt. A Controlling husband can make his wife feel guilty for not having supper on the table at exactly 6:00. A Controlling parent can maneuver her children to pursue certain careers by playing on their sense of obligation and guilt. And a Controlling pastor can put a guilt trip on his congregation for not supporting the Lord's work generously. Controllers often needle the conscience of others to get from them what they want.

Of course, a healthy relationship cannot live on a steady diet of fear and guilt. But the bottom line is that in most of their relationships, Controllers wield the power.

Self-reliance

Controllers detest teamwork and group activity. They would rather have to take a blow to the chin than admit their reliance on other people. They are proud to be rugged individualists, but their emphasis on self-reliance alienates them from other people—and leaves them feeling lonely.

The oldest living thing on our planet is the giant Sequoia tree. It has survived because it grows straight and can grow a new top if the old top is knocked off by a lightning bolt. But the most important reason for its longevity and strength is that it always grows with the support of other Sequoias. They intertwine their individual root systems and thus are able to hold one another up.

Controllers could learn a lesson from the old Sequoia. Their independence and self-reliance cause them to miss out on the benefits of interdependence. Their relational roots are shallow and they live by the maxim, "If you want it done right, do it yourself."

An Absence of Emotion

In my hospital work, I often counsel bereaved people after the death of a loved one. Some people sit across from me knowing they ought to be feeling grief or pain, but they do not feel anything because they have never learned how to let themselves feel. With the possible exception of anger and annoyance, they have never learned the language of emotions.

At funerals, I will often see an older woman crying at the top of her voice, "Why? Why did this have to happen? He was so good!" And a forty-year-old man in a three-piece suit will become very uncomfortable and say, "Can't somebody make her shut up?"

Controllers have a tough time tuning in to their emotions. Not only are they unable to feel grief, they are also unable to feel joy or excitement. Since Controllers are emotionally disengaged, they often think love is all head and no heart.

I know a stodgy, goal-oriented Controller who believes love is a choice. He did not feel love or experience love; rather, he simply did loving things as well as a robot might. But according to parish priest and counselor Morton Kelsey, "Love that is merely rationally willed and does not spring from the heart's desire is seldom love at all."[1] Love is not a bare choice or a mere act. To be effective, to communicate empathy, love must involve the heart as well as the mind.

Love as a Means, Not as an End

Controllers are not good at loving behavior. They may act polite, show consideration, and be witty, kind, and giving. However, their "love" is often unconsciously designed to make other people fall under their influence and help them accomplish their goals.

The attainment of the Controller's goal is often more

important than the route he takes to reach it. For this reason, Controllers tend to view relationships more as a means to gain more control than as an end that rests in love. Their interest in others lies in their potential usefulness to them and thus leaves some people feeling used.

"When we ask 'What can you do for me?' we have ceased to love," says John Powell.[2] Controllers don't always see it that way. They are capable of using others for their own advantage and then believing they are acting out of love. Loving someone for being an extension of your will, however, is not really love. It is just a roundabout way of loving yourself.

Rigid Rules

Controllers often seem as inflexible as a drill sergeant. They want their life to run a certain way and aren't willing to budge from their regimen. They have perfectionistic qualities with exacting ideals. They have a particular way of doing almost everything: mowing the lawn, arranging the furniture, preparing a salad, and even shopping in a mall.

In marriage, Controllers may manage all the money and demand to sign all the checks. They "know" what's best for everyone and may only "allow" others to take the reins temporarily if they don't challenge the system.

The Controller's relationships are forced to conform to his rigid reign. His strict and often unspoken rules shape relationships that accommodate his desires. While some of his relationships help him soften hard spots and sand off sharp corners, the Controller often provokes irritation.

Labeling

Controllers love labels. They help ease their anxiety by putting everything in its place, even people. Controllers often indulge in name calling—as we can see among politicians, who are often Controllers. For example, John Adams said Thomas Jefferson's mind was "eaten to a honeycomb with ambition, yet weak, confused, uninformed, and ignorant." Jefferson complained that Adams was "distrustful, obstinate, excessively vain, and takes no counsel from anyone." Harry Truman summed up Lyndon Johnson with a curt "No guts!" Likewise, Dwight Eisenhower called Johnson "superficial and opportunistic."

When faced with conflict, the Controller puts his "opponent" in a box, hoping to keep him there. Unless he is threatened to the point of losing his composure, the Controller will calmly and coolly "diagnose" a problem and prescribe its solution. "I can't reason with you if you are going to be so emotional," he will tell his tearful wife. "As soon as you calm down and get your act together I will be happy to sort things out. But you are just too emotional." For the Controller husband, labeling his wife as "emotional" is a convenient way to cut down her arguments and almost always puts her on the defensive. No one likes to be labeled.

An ancient proverb says, "A person with a bad name is already half-hanged." It is easy to be hanged by a Controller. They are smooth operators who rarely "lose" an argument.

Demanding Style of Communication

Friend: "Where would you like to go for dinner?"

Controller: "I'm in the mood for seafood and I know just the place. Can you drive?"

While the Pleaser "defers" in communication, the Controller "demands." Controllers speak with authority and rarely mince their words. Controllers make "hard commands," which offer no explanation. For example, if they saw a child about to touch a hot stove, they'd say only, "Don't touch" without telling why.

If a Pleaser's words fall as softly as rose petals, the Controller's fall like stones: "What do you mean you can't go with me? I was depending on you and you owe it to me!"

The CONTROLLER's Strengths

- highly productive
- natural problem solver
- effective leader
- confronts conflict head-on
- masterful planner and strategist
- strong ego boundaries
- visionary and motivational
- purposeful

AN EIGHT-STEP PLAN FOR CONTROLLERS

If you are a Controller, scoring low on love and low on guilt, you know the weariness and the eventual emptiness that can come from trying in vain to "rule the jungle." You also know that being in command has its advantages.

The following steps are designed to help you build on your strengths and move you from relating with your head to relating with your heart as well. They will help you complement your analytical skills with sympathy and bring you closer to true empathy.

1. Admit your deficits.

While the Pleaser has difficulty asking for help because she wants to be the helper, the Controller has difficulty asking for help because he doesn't want to admit he needs it. For the Controller, asking for help is a sign of weakness and diminishes his power. For example, if a Controller is lost, he would rather drive around for hours than stop to ask for directions.

If you are a Controller, you must be honest with yourself and admit your lack of sympathy. You will never love as well as you can until you combine an ability to sympathize with your ability to analyze. Ask trusted friends for objective feedback on your interpersonal style. Ask them: How do people perceive me? Do I convey emotion and empathy? How could I improve the way I relate to people? Tell them that you are trying to acquire an accurate picture of yourself and that you are open to criticism.

2. Practice the art of relinquishment.

You cannot change your behavior without understanding the motives behind it. You must know the why before you can change the what.

Controllers are "controlling" because they feel

insecure. They are defending themselves against anxiety by keeping a tight grip on their world.

At the risk of causing anxiety, I urge you to experiment with letting go. Try relinquishing control of a task you don't really enjoy doing in the first place. Delegate to someone a project at work or at home, and keep your hands off. Then wait and see what happens. Most likely, the project will get done—even without your interference!

Giving others control strengthens their confidence and lets them know you value their contribution. If you are always in control, you will squelch the flowering of a relationship that opens up only when others have a chance to share their unique visions. "Every great man is always being helped by everybody," said John Ruskin, "for his gift is to get good out of all things and all persons."

So empty yourself of your need to be totally in charge. You need to take a backseat from time to time. Give yourself permission to be about as influential as the "p" in pneumonia or the "k" in knitting. Bite your tongue when you have an urge to shout a command, and sit on your hands when you have an urge to pitch in.

3. Identify feelings.

G. Gordon Liddy of Watergate fame would show how tough he was by holding his hand over a burning flame. When asked, "Doesn't it hurt?" he would answer, "Of course it hurts. The trick is not to let yourself feel it."

Like Liddy, Controllers have developed their capacity to suppress pain—as well as a host of other emotions.

Feelings make them vulnerable, and Controllers reason that they are more likely to maintain the upper hand if they keep their emotions out of the picture. However, you will not be fully mature until you open yourself to your feelings. You must learn to identify your own feelings and the feelings of others in order to develop genuine empathy.

For most Controllers, dealing with feelings means learning a new vocabulary. I keep a large poster in my counseling office to use with Controllers who need a little boost when it comes to talking about feelings. It lists dozens of feeling-words. Here are a few "new" words that may help you identify your feelings: aggressive, agonized, anxious, apologetic, arrogant, bashful, blissful, bored, cautious, confident, curious, demure, determined, disappointed, disapproving, disbelieving, disgusted, ecstatic, enraged, envious, exasperated, exhausted, frightened, frustrated, grieving, guilty, happy, hurt, hysterical, indifferent, innocent, interested, jealous, joyful, lonely, meditative, mischievous, miserable, negative, obstinate, optimistic, paranoid, perplexed, prudish, puzzled, regretful, relieved, sad, satisfied, sheepish, smug, withdrawn. Whenever you are tempted to dismiss your feelings, stop and think about what you are feeling. Put a name to your emotion. Simply identifying your feelings will help you to become more comfortable with them.

4. Own responsibility.

Controllers rarely if ever admit to having been wrong, and they will go to great lengths to show that someone else is at fault. Like a peacock raising its tail feathers to scare off attackers, the Controller will put on a display of power to intimidate his opponents. Or, like a rattlesnake, he will coil and strike, killing off any opposition. With either approach, he is avoiding responsibility and walling out healthy relationships.

While the Pleaser wallows in guilt feelings, the Controller is repelled by them. In his mind, the guilty should be shot at dawn. If he dents the car, he will brush off his guilt by saying, "The car got smacked up," because he would choke on the words "I smacked up the car." And he also will say, "Her feelings got hurt," because he can't accept responsibility for hurting his wife's feelings.

Let me make this perfectly clear: it is possible to take the blame and survive. You will not be thrown in jail or strung up at dawn for confessing your faults. In fact, laying the blame on others only exacerbates your mistake and makes healthy relationships more difficult to achieve. Learn to own responsibility for things within your control and say, "I'm sorry."

5. Replace guilt motivation with love motivation.

Guilt motivation almost always backfires. But it is a quick and dirty method Controllers use to get their own way. Guilt is a Controller's tool for twisting a person's will.

Debbie, a cheerful college student, was the daughter of a guilt-inducing minister. She told me how her father would "preach" at home to whip his children into shape. "He would tell us that God sees our shameful thoughts and the nasty way we behave." When she had just as much of his guilt as she could handle, she rebelled. As a high school student she would go on drinking binges with her friends, raise a beer to her lips, and say, "Here's one for the deacons' board!"

Her experience with a guilt-inducing father who put his ministry ahead of his family gave Debbie reason to rebel. Her father's sermons created resentment rather than relationship. In other words, his sermons backfired.

Influence is like a savings account—the less you use it, the more you've got. Learn to avoid "influencing" others through guilt and shame. Instead of hitting people over the head with statements like "I can't believe you ... " or "You never ... ," motivate them with love. Communicate acceptance, forgiveness, and affirmation. Give them a vision for a better way and work together to create it. Use statements like "I'm wondering if I could give you a hand with ... " or "I appreciate your hard work and all you are doing to make this project a success." If someone seems not to accept your affirmation, don't give up. They may just need to be praised a second time.

6. *Recognize your need for others.*

People, especially Pleasers, gravitate toward Controllers like iron filings toward a magnet. They admire the Controller's influence, support his vision, and vicariously enjoy his adventures and accomplishments.

But just because you have supporters doesn't mean you recognize and rely on their support. Controllers lean toward self-sufficiency and rugged individualism. Make a conscious effort to remember how much you need other people. Remember that you are neither a rock, nor an island. Homer said, "Light is the task where many share the toil."

To heighten your awareness of your need for others, you might find it useful to use a visual symbol to serve as a remembrance. Alex Haley, the author of *Roots*, had a picture in his office showing a turtle sitting atop a fence. The picture was there to remind him of a lesson he learned early in life: "If you see a turtle on a fence post, you know he had some help," said Alex. "Any time I start thinking, *Wow, what a marvelous thing I've done!* I look at that picture and remember how this turtle, me, got up on that post."

7. Avoid quick-fire solutions.

Controllers love to solve a problem, because then they can check it off their mental to-do list and move on to something else. The difficulty with quick-fire solutions is that much of the time, a person's "solution" is found in the process of talking about their feelings, not in learning what to do.

I remember a couple who came to see me because her husband would give ready-made answers whenever the wife had a problem. Without listening to her feelings, he would quickly move to solve her problem. Eventually she began to talk more with her friends about her problems and gradually withdrew from sharing anything meaningful with her husband. He then complained that she never opened up and that he would only learn what concerned her by listening to a one-sided conversation when she talked to her friends on the phone.

Controllers use what I call bumper-sticker brush-offs to quickly dismiss a problem. "Let go and let God," they say, or "Just give it time." Instead of offering genuine support, they give one-liners.

Don't push aside another's feelings and offer quick solutions to relieve your own distress. Flip advice closes down relationships. It belittles a discontented mate, a resentful teenager, or an intimate friend. All are seeking understanding, not a bumper-sticker brush-off.

8. *Focus on persons rather than your performance.*

Do you ever find yourself wondering, "If I have it all together, why do I feel that something is missing?" Focusing on *how* we are doing rather than *who* we are robs us of meaning. Being in control and having power over people may be gratifying for a short while, but never in the long run. Ultimately it leaves us empty and lonely.

I think of billionaire Howard Hughes in his last years. He focused completely on performance, not persons, and was an expert at manipulating people to do his will. But he ended up emotionally isolated, surrounded by hired servants and favor seekers and wondering why so few people loved him.

Deep down, our souls are not hungry for fame, wealth, or power. Those rewards create as many problems as they solve. Our souls are hungry for meaning. Don't let your focus on achievement rob you of meaningful, healthy relationships. Don't hang your value on your performance.

10

Reluctant Love: The Withholder

Ted, intensely aloof but intelligent, reluctantly came to therapy on the urging of his concerned boss. Ted repaired computers in a small shop and did excellent work, but his relationships with customers and other employees were a disaster.

Studying the titles of the books on my shelf, Ted sat motionless as I began to ask some basic questions. He answered with little emotion. When I asked him about his childhood, Ted remained silent for several minutes. Then, as if to test my sincerity, he described a little of how his mother would fly into violent fits of rage. "Different things set her off—my room, for example. I tried to keep my room clean, but sometimes it just wasn't clean enough for her. I remember a day when I left for school without having made my bed," he continued. "I thought I could get home and clean it up before she saw it. But I was late, and she exploded!"

Staunchly holding back his tears, Ted described the painful incident: "She slapped me in the face, over and over. I put my arm up to protect myself, and she started screaming that I was trying to hit her! I felt so guilty. If only I had kept my room clean none of that would have happened."

As a result of being repeatedly abused by his mother, Ted came to accept a distorted view of all relationships. His unconscious goal in life is to protect himself from relational wounds. Like the Pleaser, Ted suffers from unnecessary guilt and shame. Unlike the Pleaser, however, Ted is not concerned with winning love from others. He has more or less given up on achieving love at all.

Ted grew up in a frightening world where his safety was shattered by the very person who should have been his protector. He learned that if his world were ever to be safe, it would be up to him to make it so. Not surprisingly, Ted is trying to protect himself from potential pain by scaring off people and avoiding altogether the vulnerability inherent in meaningful relationships.

Ted, like thousands of others, is a Withholder.

	High	**LOVE**	Low
High	**PLEASER** *Sympathizes*		**WITH- HOLDER** *Personalizes*
G U I L T			
Low	**LOVER** *Empathizes*		**CONTROLLER** *Analyzes*

The Withholder's Profile: The Withholder is plagued with feelings of guilt and, relatively speaking, does not place a high value on loving traits. Withholders, compared to others, do not analyze or sympathize.

WHO IS THE WITHHOLDER?

The fairy tale *Rapunzel* tells of a beautiful young girl who is imprisoned in a tower by an old witch who insists that Rapunzel is ugly. One day when Rapunzel gazes from the window of her tower, she sees her Prince Charming standing below. He is enchanted by her beauty and tells her to let her long golden tresses down from the window. The prince then braids her hair into a ladder and climbs up to rescue her.

The implicit message of this fairy tale is simple and profound. Rapunzel's prison is really not the tower but her fear that she is ugly and unlovable. The mirroring eyes of her prince, however, tell her that she is loved, and thus she is set free from the tyranny of her own imagined worthlessness.

Withholders, like Rapunzel, are enslaved by feelings of rejection. They are immobilized in their relationships by a deep sense of shame. Withholders show little concern for other people's problems and needs. They do not use their analytical ability to sort out and understand the concerns of other persons. Withholders, in fact, protect themselves by avoiding meaningful relationships altogether. And it almost always takes a sensitive and patient "Prince Charming" to break through their tough shell and release them from their isolation.

Jonah is one of the best-known Withholders.

When God called him to preach to the city of
Nineveh, Jonah up and ran away! And when a storm
threatened to capsize the boat Jonah was on, he knew
immediately whose fault the storm was. "Throw me
into the sea," he said, "and it will become calm"
(1:12). Only when he was trapped in the belly of the
great fish did Jonah stop running and face up to God.
Yet when he went to Nineveh and they repented, he
again withdrew. Sitting outside the city under a vine,
he whined and pouted. Like other Withholders, Jonah
had no empathy—much less sympathy—for the
Ninevites. God himself had to point out to Jonah that
his love extends even to those outside the Jewish
nation.

You may be a **WITHHOLDER** if . . .
- you often feel isolated and lonely
- you struggle with the capacity to trust others
- you avoid vulnerability in yourself as well as
  others
- you do not express interest in others by asking them questions
- you punish people with your silence
- you have endured unconscionable pain in
  your past
- you feel helpless to improve your relationships
- you are neither self-assertive nor self-
  sacrificial
- you are overwhelmed with a sense of not
  being good enough

In the course of my medical psychology fellowship I often consulted with physicians who were treating patients suffering from extensive physical burns. Because the healing process is lengthy and because the necessary treatment is so painful, some burn patients simply give up. As the nurses transport them into large tanks where their burned skin is meticulously scrubbed to prevent dangerous infections, these patients will scream, "Don't touch me! Just let me die!"

Similarly, Withholders suffer excruciating emotional pain and tend to give up hope of ever experiencing loving relationships. Many Withholders have grown up in homes where a parent's mood was unpredictable and his or her behavior physically abusive. Some suffered the death of a family member. Many were verbally abused with such statements as "You'll never amount to anything," "Can't you do anything right?" or "You are the most disgusting little creep who ever walked the face of the earth."

Not every Withholder is a victim of abuse. When a Pleaser burns out, for example, she will usually move into the Withholding quadrant. The Controller who has had one too many of his plans turn sour may become a Withholder. Regardless of their background, Withholders become so disillusioned or frightened by the potential pain of relationships that they fade into the woodwork, preferring the safety of their own world to the risk of relationships.

Withholders, in order to avoid any possibility of emotional pain, withdraw from relationships and through their silence send the message: "Don't touch!"

THE WITHHOLDER'S PERSONALIZING STYLE

A college student came to see me because of a frightening incident that occurred with his usually quiet roommate. "I stepped into the rest room on our floor and saw him bent over the sink, washing his face," he told me. "Then he raised his head and caught a glimpse of himself in the mirror. He stared at himself with disgust and hatred. Then he screamed at his reflection and smashed the mirror with his fist!"

This student's inner judge had pronounced the sentence, and his inner executioner had begun meting it out. He is a Withholder, someone who "personalizes" all his encounters and believes that everything that happens is his own fault. The Withholder's guilt and shame seem limitless, and the effects of that shame, while not usually as dramatic as this student's, are always devastating. The Withholder's shame and pain has so clouded his capacity to recognize his own worth as well as the value of others, that he becomes egocentric. The Withholder is not necessarily selfish, just self-focused. In a sense, he wears mirrored sunglasses with reversed lenses so all he can see as he looks out at the world is a reflection of his own pain.

This self-focus prevents the Withholder from sympathizing or analyzing. The Withholder has worked so diligently at avoiding pain that he has learned not to feel anything at all. He feels no hope, no joy, no love. He has become emotionally anesthetized. Because of his fear of being disappointed or hurt, he has chosen a life of emotional flatness. His emotions are deadened, with one major exception. He suffers the shame of toxic guilt. Only the Withholder's feelings of self-condemnation are alive and well.

If threatened enough, the Withholder's shame turns into blame. Their self-condemnation eventually reverses itself, and they lash out against others. Withholders can be downright mean. Nathan, a Withholder, was always a loner. In high school he would eat by himself in the cafeteria if no one invited him to join them, and he never went out with others on the weekend unless they initiated it. Nathan, in typical Withholding fashion, believed that he was the cause of his "rejections" and rarely blamed others. As the years went by, however, Nathan became increasingly bitter. In his forties he began resenting others for not befriending him, and he openly berated those who did not reach out to him. At the same time, he continued to punish himself. Nathan was on a spiral of compounded condemnation—condemning himself, then others, then himself some more. In fact, the harder Nathan was on himself, the meaner he became.

French novelist Albert Camus said, "The more I accuse myself, the more I have a right to judge you." Withholders like Nathan agree, at least unconsciously. And the ultimate result of their tendency to condemn themselves and others is that Withholders never enjoy sharing the love of another human heart. The Russian philosopher Nicolas Berdyaev puts it this way, "We do not know the inmost depths of the human heart; it is revealed only to love. But those who condemn have generally little love, and therefore the mystery of the heart which they judge is closed to them."

THE WITHHOLDER'S RELATIONSHIPS

The Withholder's relationships are characterized by: (1) a need to withhold, (2) self-focus, (3) helplessness, (4) caution, (5) passive aggressiveness, (6) suffering *from* rather than *with*, and (7) a defecting style of communication.

The Need to Withhold

On the surface, the Withholder may appear content. He does not express his suffering as the Pleaser, nor is he driven to achieve power like the Controller. But his calm exterior is very deceptive. Underneath it lies a legion of wounds, and the fear of being wounded again petrifies him. He walks through his days trying to avoid potential pain. He has resigned himself not to expect much from life and doesn't even bother to participate fully in life's joys. He withholds himself from others. He has ceased to hope, to dream, to wish, and to believe that anything good will ever happen to him. He is more a robot than a person. He secretly wonders why he can't be more like other people, but he shuns close relationships. To feel safe he does not allow anyone to get close enough to be a threat.

Withholders do have the capacity to relate to others, and they do participate in life to some degree. They make friends and even marry, but only with great difficulty. They have to seek out partners who are able to respect their extreme need for privacy and their need to withhold.

Working with others is also very difficult for the Withholder. Most want to be self-employed and resent working for a boss. Ted, for example, enjoyed his computer repair work, but he became irritated at even the slightest suggestion from his boss—and would sometimes ignore his boss completely. Ted became incensed if a customer questioned his assessment of a problem, and he would leave customers hanging while he went to the back of his shop to work on something else. Ted wanted to be left alone with no boss and no customers to distract or threaten him.

The Withholder's relational problems are greater than the Pleaser's or the Controller's. His suppressed self makes up the largest part of who he is, and he constantly uses up his energies to withhold from others.

Self-focus

A psychiatrist might classify the Withholder's relationships as "narcissistic." The term is derived from a mythical story about a young boy, Narcissus, who fell in love with his own image reflected in a pond and rejected everyone else.

Withholders are wrapped up in their own world, too. Unlike Narcissus, however, they are not focused on their beauty, but rather on their fear and guilt. Withholders cannot see beyond their own pain and neediness. Their self-punishment and fear of being hurt prevent them from focusing on anyone other than themselves. On the one hand, they rarely initiate contact with others, but on the other hand, they resent it when others don't initiate contact with them. Withholders can sit through an entire lunch with colleagues and never express an interest in them. They are seemingly oblivious to the fact that they are not even asking the most elementary questions of social etiquette. They invite little attention from others and disclose little themselves.

Helplessness

In an earlier chapter, I talked about the concept of learned helplessness and the fact that many of us give up even in situations where we can easily overcome the difficulties. The Withholder is especially prone to this sort of helplessness.

A Withholder is like a circus elephant that, while still young and weak, is tied with a heavy chain to an immovable iron stake. The young elephant discovers he cannot break the chain or move the stake no matter how hard he tries. Then regardless of how large and strong the elephant becomes, he continues to believe that he cannot move the stake. If he tried, however, the powerful elephant could easily escape.

Withholders are restrained by a mindset that says, "I can never improve my situation." They feel hopeless. Because of bad relationships in the past, the Withholder believes all relationships are bad. Mark Twain once said, "If a cat sits on a hot stove, that cat will never sit on a hot stove again." He continued, "That cat will never sit on a cold stove either."

Caution

Each of us has a healthy need to be cautious. We don't make serious commitments until we are certain that the person we are pledging promises to is fully trustworthy. For the Withholder, however, this need is all-consuming.

I counsel numerous college students who are looking for intimacy but are cautious of commitment. Some are so fearful of potential pain in their relationships that they will forgo the possibilities of love altogether. They view serious involvement with others as a trap that limits their options. Others want to "try out" commitment but fear they will not succeed. Some couples in premarital counseling confess that they are troubled by "the 'death do us part' thing." They fear being stuck in a relationship they won't enjoy and want a "commitment" that leaves them an exit.

Like these students, Withholders avoid relational commitments. Withholders don't trust the love of others, and they feel there must be a hook. They have a difficult time giving others the benefit of the doubt and often feel they have never been loved without someone wanting or expecting something of them. For Withholders, every relationship signals the flashing yellow light of caution.

Passive Aggressiveness

During World War II, army psychiatrist Colonel William Menninger coined the term *passive-aggressive* to refer to insubordinate soldiers who ignored and resisted orders. This phrase is now used to describe the emotional game-playing that takes place everywhere, from the boardroom to the bedroom.

Passive aggression is the crime of omission. It is sugarcoated hostility and can be very frustrating and infuriating. It occurs when the Withholder is angry and won't tell why. It occurs when he promises to be at a restaurant at 7:30 and shows up at 8:15. It occurs when his "inadvertent" barbs hurt others' feelings once too often. The Withholder is armed with an endless list of excuses to deflect responsibility for any misdeed. And in a vain attempt to rid himself of his guilt, he will turn the tables, making himself the hapless victim of your excessive demands and tirades.

Withholders are not passive one moment and aggressive the next. Because they lack the confidence to challenge or confront someone directly and calmly, their resistance comes out indirectly and covertly. They thwart others by misconstruing personal relationships as struggles in which they are powerless. The Withholder suppresses rather than resolves interpersonal conflict.

Suffer From Rather than With

Like someone who cannot keep his tongue off a sensitive tooth, Withholders get a strange, distorted pleasure in being hurt by others again and again. Withholders treasure their pain. They attempt to feel worthy and decent by suffering silently. Suffering helps them feel superior to the person they resent and gives them an excuse to hurt others by withholding their love.

Withholders do not identify well with others' suffering because they are too wrapped up in their own trials. They are busy savoring the pain others have caused them, and they have insulated themselves from feeling any obligation to suffer along with others.

Withholders keep score of hurts. They have mental

files on every person who has injured them. Their indignation toward others is etched into their memory, and they are not about to erase it. The result, of course, is further withdrawal. The irony of resentment is that it always kills the spirit of the person who wields it.

Defecting Style of Communication

> Friend: "Where would you like to go for dinner?"
> Withholder: "I don't know."
> Friend: "Are you hungry for pizza?"
> Withholder: "I don't know."
> Friend: "Let's get a deep dish with all the works."
> Withholder: "Whatever."

Withholders pout, get hurt, and sometimes slam doors. But most of all they defect. They express strong opinions from time to time, but their loudest messages are heard when they leave the room, evade questions, and retreat into silence. To most, it appears as if Withholders are not really present in conversations at all. In reality, however, they speak a powerful language of groans and sighs that are understood by a select group of colleagues, friends, and family.

Consider the following transaction between Jim, a Withholder, and his friend Sam: "Is there something wrong, Jim?"

"No," Jim whimpers.

"Are you sure?" Sam asks.

Jim nods an unconvincing "yes." As Sam walks away, he hears the sound of Jim's woeful sighs.

Interpretation: You didn't try hard enough to understand my frustration, and I'm not about to reveal anything to you until I have proof positive that you really want to know.

The Withholder's communication style relies on lots of silence. In a good relationship, silence can be relaxing, a sign that you are at home with each other. But for the Withholder, silence is a weapon. In Erica Jong's novel *Fear of Flying*, a husband and wife fight over his silence:

> "Why do you always have to do this to me? You make me feel so lonely."
>
> "That comes from you."
>
> "What do you mean it comes from me? Tonight I wanted to be happy. It's Christmas Eve. Why do you turn on me? What did I do?"
>
> Silence.
>
> "What did I do?"
>
> He looks at her as if her not knowing were another injury.

The argument continues until the husband finally goes to bed, never telling his wife what is troubling him. His refusals to tell his wife what is bothering him are like blows to his wife's dignity.

The **WITHHOLDER**'s Strengths
- contemplative and introspective
- carefully looks before leaping
- has the potential to articulate the experience of emotional pain
- knows how to survive

AN EIGHT-STEP PLAN FOR WITHHOLDERS

If you are a Withholder, scoring low on love and high on guilt, you undoubtedly know the pain of interpersonal friction. You are aware of the anxiety you often experience in relationships and your fears of being used or mistreated by others.

The following steps are designed to help you move beyond your fear and guilt to enjoy the delights of healthy interpersonal connections.

1. Admit your deficit.

You are probably motivated more by fear and guilt than you are by love. Your desire for self-protection and your lack of self-worth keep you from receiving and giving the gift of love. This is the root of your relational struggles, and little can be done to improve your situation until you face this deficit of love head on.

Love is a central condition of human existence. We need it for survival. We seek it for pleasure. We require it to lend meaning and purpose to our lives. Love is not an embellishment or a refinement on the human condition. It is not the icing on the cake; it *is* the cake.

You can overcome your deficit of love by trying to understand the people around you. As S. I. Hayakawa said, "It is only as we fully understand opinions and attitudes different from our own and the reasons for them that we better understand our own place in the scheme of things." You have the capacity to give and receive love; you simply need to learn how to tap into it. The remaining steps will help you do so.

2. Plug into a caring community.

A caring community is a powerful healing and growth agent. An African proverb says, "It takes a whole village to raise a child." It also takes a whole community to raise a Withholder to a more positive level of relationships. Your struggles cannot be worked out in isolation. A group of caring people is needed to model and foster healthy relationships.

When a retarded child is born, Professor Stanley Hauerwas of Duke University has written, the religious question we should ask is not "Why does God permit mental retardation in his world?" but "What sort of a community should we become so that mental retardation need not be a barrier to a child's enjoying a gratifying life?" In the same way, you need to ask yourself what kind of community will best encourage you to grow.

Life's toughest struggles are eased in a caring community of loving people. While relationships admittedly cause us problems, they also bring us our greatest joy. Make an effort to involve yourself in a group of positive people. Join a club or attend a class in your church or neighborhood. A caring community will help you recognize that other people may complicate your existence, but without them life is unbearably desolate.

3. Beware of your defenses.

Achilles, the Greek mythological hero, was noted for his strength and bravery. When he was still a baby, his mother, Thetis, had a premonition that he would die in battle. So, holding Achilles by the heel, she dipped him in the River Styx to make him invulnerable.

As fate would have it, a poison arrow shot by Apollo wounded Achilles in the heel, his only vulnerable spot, and caused his death.

The Withholder seeks to be invulnerable. He wears psychological defenses like a suit of armor. It is all in vain, however. Everyone has a weak spot. Everyone has an "Achilles' heel."

When your primary concern is with maximum security, you will soon find yourself living in a prison. The anxiety and guilt you carry unconsciously drive you to protect yourself from others. Robert Frost gives helpful advice to Withholders: "Do not build a wall until you know what you are walling in and what you are walling out."

Whether you are aware of it or not, you are instinctively building walls between you and other people. The bricks in your wall include the defenses of denial, projection, and repression. Beware of these psychological maneuvers and how you may be using them to avoid responsibility for your condition.

Love has no defenses. Only after you begin to break down your psychological walls will you realize your full potential for enjoying love and life.

4. Focus on the needs of others.

There is an old Chinese tale about a woman whose only son died. In her grief, she went to a holy man and said, "What magical incantations do you have to bring my son back to life?" Instead of sending her away or reasoning with her, he said to her, "Fetch me a mustard seed from a home that has never known sorrow. We will use it to drive the sorrow out of your life."

The woman set off at once in search of that magical mustard seed. She came first to a splendid mansion, knocked at the door, and said, "I am looking for a home that has never known sorrow. Is this such a place?" They told her, "You've certainly come to the wrong place," and began to describe all the tragic things that had recently befallen them. The woman said to herself, "Who is better able to help these poor unfortunate people than I, who have had misfortune of my own?" She stayed to comfort them, then went on in her search for a home that had never known sorrow. But wherever she turned, in hovels and palaces, she found one report after another of sadness and misfortune. Ultimately, the woman became so involved in ministering to other people's grief that she forgot about her quest for the magical mustard seed, never realizing she had in fact driven the sorrow out of her life.

You will only transcend your own pain by attending to the pain that others carry. Look beyond your own neediness and attend to the needs of others.

5. Find compassionate but honest feedback.

Henry Ward Beecher said, "No man can tell another his faults so as to benefit him, unless he loves him." If you are to climb over your defensive walls and learn to empathize with others, you will need a trusted guide, a mentor that will make the journey with you.

Ask yourself who has had the most positive influence in your life. Is it a schoolteacher? An aunt or uncle? A parent? A grandparent? A minister? An employer? A coach? Whoever it is, your reason for choosing this person probably has more to do with who they are and how they live than anything else.

While finding a mentor may be difficult, an empathetic mentor could be the key to your quest to attain wholeness. Approach the person you respect and ask him or her to be in a mentoring relationship that would enable you to learn more about love. As a mentoree, of course, you will need to open yourself to critical feedback. But a true mentor will give you compassionate feedback and provide accountability to help you improve.

Even Ebenezer Scrooge had a "mentor" in Jacob Marley's ghost. As a result of their relationship, the miserly old man exclaimed, "I will not be the man I was!" And indeed, he changed his ways and became for the first time in his life open to love and relationships.

6. Risk vulnerability.

There is no way around it: caring for others leaves us vulnerable to disappointment and rejection. Relationships are risky. Just as a child risks scraping a knee in climbing a tree, so do you and I risk emotional pain when we enter a relationship.

There is no way we can live a rich life unless we are willing to suffer grief, sadness, anger, agony, confusion, criticism, and rejection. As psychiatrist and author M. Scott Peck has said, "We cannot heal without being willing to be hurt."[1]

Dr. Peck also said, "If Jesus taught us anything, he taught us that the way to salvation lies through vulnerability."[2] Take the risk of opening yourself to another person. Disclose your pain to someone (like your mentor). The effect of vulnerability on others is almost always disarming. When we gird ourselves with psychological defenses and pretend to be something we are not, the people around us become defensive as well. When you are vulnerable, however, it sends a message of authenticity and invites people to disclose their fears and pains too. Vulnerability is the bridge into a genuine caring relationship and will lead you over the troubled waters of withholding.

7. Rid yourself of guilt and shame.

In Chapters 5 and 6, I outlined the basic strategies for resolving true guilt and false guilt. Remember that guilt and shame are at the root of your relational struggles. Don't expect to break free from patterns of withholding until you have exorcised the demon of shame.

8. Seek healing through professional help.

Every Withholder can benefit from the objective help of a trained psychotherapist or counselor. One of the best ways to locate a competent therapist is to ask others in the helping profession if they know of a good counselor. Physicians, ministers, nurses, and teachers often provide excellent referrals. Other informational sources include hospitals, community service societies, referral services, and local professional societies.

If you have grown up with painful memories that have never been resolved, I urge you to seek professional help. This final step may be the most important thing you do for yourself and the people in your life.

11

Authentic Love:
The Lover

Renee, in her thirties, hadn't seen her younger sister, Suzanne, for more than a year. Renee had been teaching English as a second language in Asia and returned home to Chicago for Christmas.

Renee was actually dreading the holidays with her sister. They had never really gotten along, and their relationship always seemed tense.

But this time it was different. To Renee's surprise, she found herself enjoying her sister's company. They took Suzanne's two children for lunch in the Walnut Room at Marshall Field's department store in the Loop. They waited in line to see Santa. They looked at toys. All the while, Renee stared in amazement as she watched Suzanne care lovingly for her children.

At home that evening while Suzanne was preparing dinner, Renee asked Suzanne's husband, Doug, "What's happened to Suzanne? I've never seen her so relaxed and warm. She seems so . . . "

"So comfortable?" Doug suggested.

"Yes. She used to be tense and overextended and smothering."

Doug's face lit up. "I know. To be honest, our marriage was barely hanging on about a year ago. Then we decided to get help, and it has really made a difference. I try to listen better and not to be so bossy, and she has learned to give me space and not be so hard on herself. Both of us feel more secure and at peace. We work hard to understand each other accurately and not jump to conclusions. We have never been happier."

That night after dinner, Renee and Suzanne cleaned up the kitchen. "I've got to tell you Suz, I'm really proud of you. You're really a great mom—and a great sister too!"

Suzanne beamed. "Thank you," she said. "You know, for the first time in my life, I'm able to accept myself and everybody around me!"

Suzanne, like thousands of other wonderful people, has become a Lover.

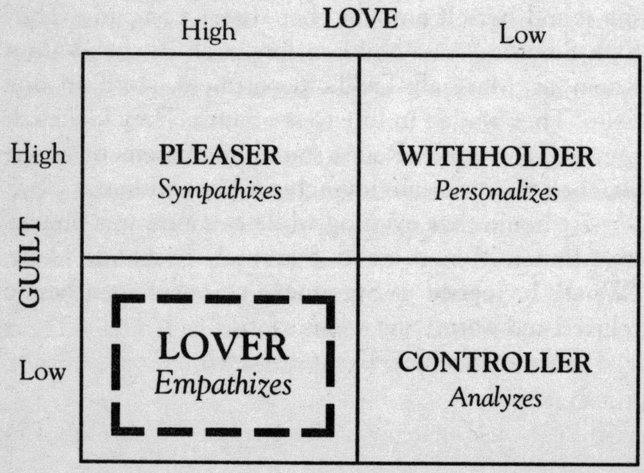

	LOVE	
	High	Low
High	**PLEASER** *Sympathizes*	**WITHHOLDER** *Personalizes*
Low	**LOVER** *Empathizes*	**CONTROLLER** *Analyzes*

GUILT (vertical axis label, left side)

The Lover's Profile: Lovers are not plagued with feelings of guilt but place a high value on loving traits. Lovers combine their capacity to analyze and sympathize in order to create genuine empathy. They love with both their heads and their hearts.

WHO IS THE LOVER?

Lovers know the difference between guilt and godly sorrow. They do not condemn themselves needlessly, and their freedom from guilt empowers them to accept others without judging them. Lovers are able to transcend their own neediness in order to serve the needs of others.

The defining feature of Lovers is their ability to treat people as people, not as a means to achieve their own ends. Pleasers see others as a means for getting guilt off their backs and increasing their good feelings about themselves. Controllers see others as a means to helping them accomplish their goals and purposes. Withholders see others as the way to nowhere but pain. But Lovers see others as ends in themselves, and this attitude equips them to become better Lovers.

Theologian Martin Buber taught that relationships take one of two forms. In the "I-It" relationship, we treat others as objects, or see them only in terms of what they can do for us. But in the "I-Thou" relationship, we see others as persons whose needs and feelings are to be respected as much as one's own. The I-Thou relationship hinges on a capacity to *transcend* self, not punish it.

Jesus, of course, was the perfect Lover. But his

mother, Mary, and father, Joseph, also demonstrated great love. Knowing she faced great ridicule and suffering, Mary still sacrificed a quiet, happy life with Joseph to become the mother of Jesus. And Joseph, out of his love for Mary and for the Lord, married her quietly, refrained from sexual relations with her until Jesus was born, and protected the young family from Herod's wrath. Mary and Joseph, like many other believers throughout history, became better Lovers when they were touched by the transforming power of God's love.

You may be a **LOVER** if . . .

- you listen for the unspoken feelings behind a person's message.
- you objectively assess a situation before jumping to conclusions.
- you realize you cannot make everyone happy.
- you enjoy receiving from others without feeling indebted.
- you are not obsessed with what others think of you.
- you put yourself in others' shoes.
- you are aware of your own needs but are also sensitive to others.
- you do not use blame or intimidation to get your own way.
- you deal with conflict openly and maturely.

The famous inscription at the Delphic oracle says: "Know thyself." Shakespeare wrote: "This above all: to thine own self be true, and it must follow, as the night the day, thou canst not then be false to any man." From earliest times serious thinkers have known that we cannot have inner peace until we know and accept who we are.

Sociologists use the word *anomie* for the sense of losing who we are. *Anomie* is the feeling of dangling in the spiritual winds, unattached to the cultural institutions, family, or group traditions and behavioral norms that give people the quiet feeling of peace in who they are, where they come from, and to whom they belong.

Lovers do not live in anomie. They are aware of their limitations. They do not cover their weaknesses with a security blanket of defense mechanisms. They know they are not always good lovers. They are aware of their selfish wants and egocentric desires.

But Lovers do not embrace a self-defeating pattern of personal condemnation. Compared to others who botch their attempts to be loving, the Lovers' approach is as inspiring as it is rare. The Pleaser is self-sacrificing. The Controller is self-assertive. The Withholder is self-centered. But the Lover is self-transcending.

"Transcend" does not mean "condemn," "obliterate," or "demolish." It literally means to "climb over." Lovers "climb over" themselves. They give not to receive, but to meet the needs of others. Lovers do not love in order to be loved, but because loving is for them a way of life. They do not try to achieve a static condition of love that can be observed, approved, and applauded. Rather, they find fulfillment in the *process* of learning to love.

Lovers recognize the importance of self-esteem, respect, and human dignity. They understand the negative consequences of self-doubt and self-hate. They are also aware of the meaninglessness of individualism, and they are committed to the common good. As British diplomat Horace Mann wrote, "He who never sacrificed a present to a future good, or a personal to a general one, can speak of happiness only as the blind do of colors."

THE LOVER'S EMPATHETIC STYLE

Lovers' minds are not clouded by feelings of guilt, and their hearts are not weighed down with shame. Because they are not preoccupied with self-condemnation, they have the capacity for full-fledged empathy. The Lover's empathetic style leads to compassionate action that transcends self-centered motivations.

Lovers offer more than sympathy or analytical problem solving: they offer empathy. They strive to understand another's distress before relieving it. Their motivation to love is not getting a reward or gaining relief from pain. It is an end, in and of itself.

Daniel Batson at the University of Kansas once conducted an experiment to demonstrate the difference between sympathy and empathy.[1] As he showed a group of people a video of a distressed woman who appeared to be receiving shocks, he told them that the woman did not suffer actual physical pain from the shocks; rather, she was terrified because as a child she had had a traumatic experience of shock.

After seeing the tape, the viewers were asked to fill out a questionnaire that measured the degree to which they had experienced distress at the woman's pain. The questionnaire also measured the degree to which they felt empathy for the woman. Dr. Batson then divided the viewers into two types: those experiencing more distress than empathy, and those experiencing more empathy than distress. In other words, he divided them into "Pleasers" and "Lovers."

Then, to determine how empathy affects behavior, Dr. Batson met with half of each group and told them they would watch as the victim received another series of shocks. But they were offered an option: they could switch places with the victim. Not surprisingly, a substantial number of both Pleasers and Lovers agreed to take the victim's place.

Dr. Batson then met with the other half of each group. He told this group they would not be seeing the victim's trials, but they too were offered the option of volunteering to switch places.

The results highlighted the crucial difference between Pleasers and Lovers. Pleasers, who operate only out of sympathy, did not have the Lovers' capacity for empathy. Almost invariably, the Pleasers who did not have to watch the woman suffer chose not to switch places with her. However, the Pleasers who would have had to watch her suffer did choose to take her place—but only to relieve their own distress at viewing her pain. The Lovers, in contrast, volunteered to take the woman's place even when they did not have to watch her suffer. Because they were empathetic, they were more concerned about the victim's terror than their own distress.

	PLEASER *Sympathizes*	**LOVER** *Empathizes*
Told they would watch as victim received shocks	*Agreed to take victim's place*	*Agreed to take victim's place*
Told they would not watch as victim received shocks	*Declined to take victim's place*	*Agreed to take victim's place*

As this experiment demonstrates, the Lover's heart pulls him or her in ways the Pleaser, Controller, and Withholder cannot comprehend. Lovers rise above their own needs and concerns. They can and do place themselves fully in the place of another. Their guilt-free minds make it possible for them to stand in someone else's place, feel as she feels, and think as she thinks.

THE LOVER'S RELATIONSHIPS

The Lover's relationships are characterized by: (1) authenticity, (2) vulnerability, (3) declarative style of communication, (4) self-transcending actions, and (5) acceptance of personal limits.

Authenticity

Margery Williams's *The Velveteen Rabbit* is about a

toy rabbit who wants to be real. "What is real?" asks the Rabbit one day. "Does it mean having things that buzz inside you and a stick-out handle?" The Skin Horse replies, "Real isn't how you are made. It's a thing that happens to you. When a child loves you for a long, long time, not just to play with, but really loves you, then you become Real."

The cornerstone of every Lover's relationship is natural authenticity. Like the toy rabbit, Lovers are on a quest to be real. Lovers do not perform under a guise that masks insincere intentions. They are genuinely concerned about the needs of the person receiving their love.

George Burns told an acting class at UCLA that the most important quality of an actor is sincerity. "And if you can fake sincerity," he said, "you've got it made." But you can't fake sincerity—at least, not for long. Sincerity flows naturally out of guilt-free love.

I spent six years in graduate school learning, watching, and imitating the professionals who practice psychotherapy. Before I graduated, one of my clinical supervisors who had studied my therapeutic skills through one-way mirror observations, dozens of video-taped sessions, and through reading verbatim transcripts of my therapy gave me some advice about being an authentic clinician. "Les," he told me, "authenticity can only exist when you stop wanting to imitate someone else. You will become a more effective psychologist as you allow yourself to be you."

Being real is what separates the Lover from the person who wants to be *seen* as loving. Authenticity is the distinguishing mark of the Lover's relationships. Lovers are not trying to be something they are not.

They are not a zirconium diamond contrived from fake materials, trying to pass for the real thing. They have stepped beyond imitation to discover authenticity.

Sincerity is found in at least three human qualities:

1. Absence of Pretense

Lovers are not overly concerned about the impression they make on others. Instead of asking "How am I doing?" they wonder "How are *they* doing?" This fundamental shift in focus from self to others relieves pretense and fosters authenticity. What they are, and what they say they are, are highly congruent.

2. Genuine Feelings

Lovers reveal their honest emotions. They do not conjure up "appropriate" emotions to play the loving part. They admit to themselves their feelings of fear, intimidation, rejection, and so on. Lovers do not ask, "What *should* I be feeling?" Instead, they ask, "What *am* I feeling?"

3. Consistent Behavior

Lovers do loving things when no one is watching. They are the same people behind the curtains as they are on stage. They do not perform in loving ways for those they hope will reward them, then act rude to safe targets, people who can't strike back. Their love is based on their values, not their audience.

Vulnerability

In Margery Williams's story, the toy rabbit didn't know real rabbits existed. He thought they were all stuffed with sawdust like himself. "And he understood that sawdust was quite out-of-date and should never be mentioned in modern circles." The Rabbit kept authenticity at bay through his fear of vulnerability.

Love is not authentic unless it comes from an open and wounded heart. Everyone's heart has been wounded. But most people would rather protect their wounds than divulge them. Lovers, however, make personal wounds available to others as a source of healing.

No one has written more sensitively on the gift of vulnerability than Henri Nouwen in his book, *The Wounded Healer*. He points out that "making one's own wounds a source of healing, does not call for a sharing of superficial personal pains but for a constant willingness to see one's own pain and suffering as rising from the depth of the human condition."[2]

Many people are constantly trying to be so sensational that others *have* to love them. Lovers, however, do not pretend to have it all together. They do not present themselves as being in complete control of their lives. They share their imperfections, problems, inadequacies, brokenness, and pain.

To be vulnerable you do not have to be a doormat. Love is not devoid of all pride. Lovers do not live behind plateglass windows so others may see every personal fault and weakness. Rather, being vulnerable means being strong enough to be who we really are. It means allowing others to see our strengths and weaknesses without our being defensive or embarrassed.

Daring acts of vulnerability serve as bridges to authentic love. In the movie *All of Me*, the characters Edwina and Roger are embroiled in a heated argument until Edwina discloses an embarrassing truth. "I don't have any friends," she tells Roger. "I'm looking back at an entire lifetime and don't have one friend. I never had any friends. I've had only nannies and tutors and servants and nurses." Roger, speechless, stares at her, his anger suddenly dissolved.

Edwina's vulnerability brings kindness and depth to the couple's relationship. They begin to share with each other their deepest hopes and fears. The film demonstrates a powerful psychological dynamic: Vulnerability begets vulnerability from others.

Vulnerability puts us in emotional jeopardy, but Lovers know it is only among the overtly imperfect that love blossoms.

Declarative Style of Communication

Friend: "Where would you like to go for dinner?"

Lover: "I'm in the mood for seafood. What about you?"

Because Lovers are able to communicate their desires, they eliminate the guesswork from conversation. They take responsibility for choices and feelings. They explore options, explain comments, compromise their desires, and negotiate their needs.

Lovers use "I" messages to clarify wishes, wants, and concerns. They do not put people on the defensive by saying "You did this" or "You did that." Instead, they couch their desires in personal terms: "I feel frustrated because I feel I'm not getting my point across." "I" messages are difficult to argue with because the person is simply saying what he or she feels.

Using "I messages," Lovers send clear, direct statements. They do not blame the other person or avoid the issue. When conflicts develop, they focus on the here and now and do not bring up old issues from the past. Lovers accept conflict and do not minimize or avoid it. Instead, they resolve conflict quickly and move on.

Let's review. The Pleaser *defers*. The Controller *demands*. The Withholder *defects*. But the Lover *declares*. However, Lovers do more than send clear messages. They are also excellent listeners, able to translate even the messages that are disguised or silent. As Elbert Hubbard said, "He who does not understand your silence will probably not understand your words."

When Jesus met the Samaritan woman at the well, he told her to call her husband. "I have no husband," the woman replied. But Jesus knew the truth that her words disguised. Gently, he said to her, "You are right when you say you have no husband. The fact is, you have had five husbands, and the man you now have is not your husband. What you have just said is quite true" (John 4:17–18).

Notice Jesus' communication style. He did not attack her, preach at her, or condemn her. Instead, he *listened* to the hidden message behind the woman's words. Then he *restated* and *interpreted* her words. And he ended by *affirming* what she had said.

Finally, Jesus listened for the feelings behind the woman's words. He sensed that she was ashamed of her lifestyle, and so she withheld the truth. Sensitive to her feelings of shame, Jesus responded with both truth and understanding.

Lovers develop a sensitivity to the feelings behind words and respond with wisdom and understanding. They listen not only to the semantic meaning of a message, but to the hidden emotional message as well.

Self-Transcending Actions

Lovers know that authentic love is often achieved when a radical price is paid, even a personal "crucifixion" of selfishness. Perhaps the most paradoxical statement Jesus ever made was, "Whoever wants to save his life will lose it, but whoever loses his life for me and for the gospel will save it" (Mark 8:35). Only through sacrificing our self-centeredness can we fully accept others as they are.

Lovers crucify their selfish attitudes. They rid themselves of unreal expectations and false preconceptions that exclude others from their circle of love. Lovers empty the self of its egoism and of its compulsive urge to change, control, or rescue others. This emptiness allows Lovers to make room in their heart for others and to appreciate their uniqueness.

Appreciation of differences allows Lovers the freedom to enjoy the good fortune of others. When we are full of ourselves, we become jealous of others. But when we empty ourselves, we are at last free to value other people. Their dreams and plans become important to us. For the first time their attractiveness, intelligence, wit, charm, and talents become beautiful gifts to enrich our lives. We rejoice with their successes, and we feel genuine sorrow at their failures.

Self-transcendence also means going the extra mile. When Jesus said, "If someone forces you to go one mile, go with him two miles" (Matt. 5:41), he was referring to the Roman practice of forcing bystanders to carry their soldiers' packs. Because they were more civilized than other armies, the Romans required them to carry the packs only one mile. However, you can be sure that once that mile was over, no Jew would walk a foot further!

Many people approach relationships with the idea of the dutiful mile. They do what is required, and no more. But Lovers do more than others expect. They turn ordinary feelings of compassion into extraordinary expressions of love.

Lovers recognize that authentic love is more than a feeling. If love were merely emotion, it would require only a minimum investment. After all, feelings of love flow as easily as adrenaline. But feelings of love never walk beyond the first mile. Authentic love, in contrast, is based on commitment to the good of the other. It does not just *feel*. It *takes action*.

If love were built merely on feelings, God might have looked at his people and said: "How miserable they must be! I hate to see them suffering. I hope they know how much I love them." But God did more than agonize. He took action by coming to earth as a human being. He healed people's hurts. He repaired broken bodies. He forgave people whether they deserved it or not. And ultimately, he died on the cross for their sins.

Lovers see the needs of others and *do* something about them.

Acceptance of Personal Limits

Mother Teresa's extraordinary love for the rejected and dying in Calcutta is known worldwide. When asked about her great compassion, she often says, "We can do no great things; only small things with great love."

Lovers aspire to the greatness of authentic love. But they do so with keen awareness and personal acknowledgment of their human limits. They realize that they have needs, drives, rights, and goals that do not easily harmonize with authentic love. Lovers, while striving to match the model of Christ's love, have given up on being human messiahs.

Adres Nygren's classic book, *Agape and Eros*, contrasts eros, which is "acquisitive desire," with agape, which is "sacrificial giving." C. S. Lewis called eros "need-love" and agape "gift-love."

Agapic love is the unconditional love modeled by God through Jesus Christ. Agapic love reaches out with no expectation of reward. It is unilateral and totally sacrificial. Agapic love never asks what can I get, but only what can I give. Agapic love does not give in the hope of inspiring another to give in return. It gives because there is a need to be met.

Eros, on the other hand, asks not what can I *give*, but what can I *get* in return for what I give. Eros is human love. We are all driven by an insatiable need to be loved. We need others and are incomplete in ourselves. We need the reward of being loved in return for giving our love. Eros is born of our human need to be whole.

Agape is the power that moves us to satisfy the needs of another, while eros is the power that drives us to seek another to satisfy our own deepest needs. Lovers do not praise agape in order to make eros look ungodly. They accept the strength and support of both.

We do not and cannot live by agapic love alone, for we are not God. Rather, we are severely limited creatures trying to manage our lives within the boundaries of human frailty. We are capable of sacrificial acts, but only when they fulfill our subconscious needs. In *The Road Less Traveled*, Dr. M. Scott Peck says, "Whatever we do for someone else we do because it fulfills a need we have."[3]

Agapic love does its work within the human limits created by eros. It slips into the crevices of our self-interest and filters through our deepest unmet needs. Agapic love does not destroy our ego but transforms it. Jonathan Edwards captured the work of agape when he said, "In some sense the most benevolent, generous person in the world seeks his own happiness in doing good to others, because he places his happiness in their good. His mind is so enlarged as to take them, as it were, into himself."

The widespread notion that love must be free from self-interest is a benign enemy of authentic love. Human attempts to give agape without eros can destroy relationships. When we focus exclusively on self-sacrifice, we turn love into law and lose the grace it is designed to bring. Our labor of love becomes a labor of legalism. Our love becomes a duty.

Lewis Smedes put it this way: "If we perceive Christian love only as lofty obligation we will be crushed by it, for agape by itself is an impossible ideal. We never manage life exclusively by self-giving love."[4]

Who but God is competent for agape's ideal? Lovers who strive to reach beyond the limits of eros will walk the extra mile in secret. But when, in their weakness, they cannot walk the extra mile, they will not condemn themselves.

Lovers understand that every human act of love is crisscrossed with both selfish and self-sacrificing motives. They live, more or less comfortably, with a paradox. On the one hand, they work to transcend their selfishness; on the other hand, they know they will never be perfect Lovers. They accept their limitations and do not condemn themselves for them, because they know they are in the process of learning to become better Lovers. As Paul writes, "Not that I have already obtained all this, or have already been made perfect, but I press on to take hold of that for which Christ Jesus took hold of me . . . forgetting what is behind and straining toward what is ahead, I press on toward the goal" (Phil. 3:12–14).

BECOMING A BETTER LOVER

Few relationships measure up to the above characteristics. In my research, Pleasers, Controllers, and Withholders outnumber Lovers. In fact, only twenty-five percent of the population are Lovers. But I have also learned in my counseling practice that people can learn to be better Lovers. I have seen Pleasers become more forthright. I have watched Controllers become more sensitive. I have witnessed Withholders break out of their shell. And I have seen Lovers become better Lovers.

In Part Three, we will look at how genuine love can transform our most important relationships. We will see how our patterns of relating affect our friendships, our marriages, our families, our jobs, and our relationship with God, and we will learn how to get along with other people who may be Pleasers, Controllers, or Withholders.

Part Three

~

BUILDING HEALTHY RELATIONSHIPS

12

That's What Friends Are For

What most people call their "circle of friends" more closely resembles a triangle. Many people have contact with between 500 and 2500 acquaintances each year, representing the base of the triangle. Then there are the 20 to 100 "core friends" in the middle. These we know by first name, and we see them somewhat regularly. At the top of the triangle are one to seven intimate friends. These people are closely involved in our lives, and their names are likely engraved on our hearts.

Friends make a difference in both our physical and emotional health. Studies have shown, for example, that people with strong friendships have healthier immune systems, lower levels of cholesterol, and live longer. Studies at the Carnegie Institute of Technology reveal that persons who develop strong friendships are more likely to be successful in their business.

The real value of friends is not found in lab studies or in a profitable bottom line, but in the sense of belonging that nurtures our existence. Each of us needs to be connected to a tightly knit group. We want to be known and accepted. We want to know that someone can be counted on to come to our rescue when we are in a jam.

But, as in all relationships, love's silent killer can break through the tightest bonds and destroy the most long-standing friendship.

HOW GUILT CUTS THE HEART OUT OF FRIENDSHIP

"I want to be a good friend, but no matter how much I do for Jackie, I just can't please her," a woman confided in me. When guilt moves silently into a friendship, it undermines the relationship. As Gary Inrig wrote in his book *Quality Friendship*, "If a friendship is not solidly based, it either will not last or it will drag us down."

In Part Two, we defined four types of people: the Pleaser, Controller, Withholder, and Lover. Before we consider how to relate to each type of person, let's briefly review their characteristics within the context of friendship. As you read the following descriptions, think about your own relationships. Are you sometimes a Controller and sometimes a Pleaser? Do you know someone who is a Withholder? Is there someone with whom you share a truly loving friendship? Because we live in a fallen world and are ourselves imperfect people, our friendships will very likely cover a range of styles.

The Compulsive Friend

The Pleaser—high on guilt and high on love—is cheerful, affectionate, seldom quarrels, and appears to be universally liked. They seem to enjoy an abundance of meaningful relationships. But paradoxically, the Pleaser, who doesn't have an enemy in the world, rarely enjoys the fulfillment of deep friendships.

The Pleaser believes their friendships will flourish if they make others happy. They suppress anger, hide fatigue, and disguise depression in a self-defeating attempt to keep their friendships alive. For this reason, Pleasers are popular. But as Alan Loy McGinnis has said in *The Friendship Factor*, "popularity is not synonymous with intimacy."[1] Intimacy is achieved through authenticity, not through popularity. Authenticity risks rejection, but popularity never takes the chance.

Pleasers, in a desperate attempt to avoid all rejection, assume unnecessary responsibility for the happiness of their friends. And when their friends are not happy the Pleaser feels guilty. Their guilt then strips them of their capacity for empathy. Without empathy they become overwhelmed by other people's problems. Their heart aches to help their friends, but their head does not offer guidance. Because Pleasers are afraid to look into the dark regions of their own repressed emotions, they lose themselves in the struggles of others. Until they deal with their own problems, Pleasers are doomed to shallow friendships and very little personal fulfillment.

The Controlling Friend

The Controller, who is low on guilt and low on love, values friendship for its advantages. The Controller evaluates relationships as a breeder examines the value of a horse, saying, "What's it worth to me?"

Controllers analyze potential friendships in terms of their conditions and worth. The more useful people are to his purposes the more likely the Controller is to befriend them.

Controllers know how to win friends and manipulate people. Their network is more important than their relationships. They manage their friendships like an investment banker does a financial portfolio. Friends are a commodity to be periodically reviewed and traded from time to time for greater return. The Controller's friendships are here today and gone tomorrow. When friends are no longer of value, they are put in storage for possible future use.

Franklin D. Roosevelt was a Controller. He made lots of friends, but only with people who could help him accomplish his goals. Historians have described him as a man without deep commitment to anyone. He enjoyed people, but he rarely gave himself to them.

Controllers conceal their vulnerable emotions and don't share personal struggles. A Controller believes that vulnerability weakens his control.

The Reluctant Friend

The Withholder, high on guilt and low on love, has great difficulty expressing or accepting intimacy in friendship. Lacking empathy, Withholders build thick and impenetrable walls. They may have friendly acquaintances with people they see on a regular basis. But they do not have a circle of close, supportive, special friends with whom they feel comfortable.

Withholders rationalize their lack of friendships by believing no one can be trusted. "Give people an inch and they will take a mile," they say. Their real fear, however, is rejection. In an attempt to avoid emotional pain, they keep deep friendship from developing by avoiding necessary losses and vulnerable risks.

Since Withholders are looking for signals of distrust, they often find them whether the signs are real or only imagined. Withholders read volumes into a nonchalant glance or the innocuous clearing of the throat. William James said that the essence of friendship is to know what to overlook. Withholders don't understand that idea. No one is trustworthy and they have huge files of mental notes to prove it.

The Authentic Friend

Lovers, low on guilt and high on love, have the empathy needed to keep friendships alive and well. They offer their friends understanding and acceptance, and they listen carefully for their friends' hidden messages. Lovers are not perfect. They may grow too busy for their friends sometimes, or they may occasionally fall into Pleasing, Controlling, or Withholding patterns. But on the whole, Lovers aim for authenticity and are not handicapped by prolonged bouts with guilt.

Greg Smith is one of my closest friends. We now live a thousand miles apart, but all through grade school we were inseparable. We were together at church, at cub scouts and camp, in our backyard forts, or fishing in Sailor's Pond. We had the same tastes: macaroni and cheese at his house, pancakes at mine. Our clothes came from the same stores, and we were often mistaken for twins. I can't imagine two boys being better buddies.

One summer at Camp Idlewild in New Hampshire, Greg and I were playing on two huge ropes that swung out over the lake. Greg asked me to stay on shore while he did a solo jump. For some reason, though, I leaped onto my rope as Greg swung out over the water. Not realizing he was going to keep hold of his rope instead of jumping, I collided with him as I swung out, my bony knees socking him right in the ribs. He fell into the water, the wind knocked out of him. He struggled back to shore in terrible pain. There, a camp counselor took over.

I felt terrible, too, but I wasn't about to let Greg know that (a common strategy for third-grade guilt). That night at dinner, when Greg came to sit by me, I said sarcastically, "You're not sitting here, are you?"

Greg sat down. "I know you've got to be feeling rotten," he told me. "Don't worry about what happened today. It was no big deal."

I couldn't believe what I was hearing. *Hey,* I thought, *he's not mad at me!*

Greg pushed his green beans into his paper napkin to save for the squirrels. "Wouldn't camp be cool if it had macaroni and cheese?" He smiled as he spoke.

Greg had extended unconditional grace to a friend, third-grade style. I didn't know it then, and neither did Greg, but grace like that keeps love's unseen enemy at bay and makes friendships last for years.

Lovers enjoy long-lasting, intimate friendships because they have transcended the fear of rejection, the need to please other people, and any tendency to use others for their own personal advantage.

DEALING WITH DIFFICULT FRIENDS

The English word *friend* springs from the same Indo-European root as the word *freedom*. The root word for *friend* means "to love," and those whom we love we set free. We set friends free from the mockery of superficial connections, the isolation of anxiety, and the dreadful fear of loneliness. A good friend sets another friend free from pleasing, controlling, and withholding patterns of relating.

Assuming that you have recognized and dealt with your own tendencies to please, control, or withhold from your friends, what do you do when one of your friends turns out to be a Pleaser, Controller, or Withholder? Here are a few pointers on befriending difficult people.

How to Befriend a Pleaser

Pleasers are prone to relate to others superficially and need a friend who is willing to plunge beneath the surface and point out their pleasing behavior patterns. They need friends who are sensitive and caring but also forthright and honest.

Cicero said, "It appears that genuine friendship cannot exist where one of the parties is unwilling to hear the truth and the other is equally indisposed to speak it." In speaking the truth to a Pleaser, however, be careful not to burden their already heavy conscience. If they never seem to let you buy lunch, for example, don't clobber them with guilt. Use "I" statements to convey your feelings. Say, for example, "Since I never get to buy you lunch, our relationship sometimes feels out of balance for me. Do you ever feel that way?"

Telling the truth to a Pleaser is always risky, but it is a sign of respect. You will never build an authentic friendship with a Pleaser unless you risk the possibility of losing the friendship altogether.

Telling the truth to a Pleaser is a sign of respect. It shows that you care about the friendship. Keeping the truth from a Pleaser demeans her. It says she is not mature enough to be trusted with reality.

Practice the fine art of telling the truth to a Pleaser and you will forge a meaningful friendship.

How to Befriend a Controller

It is not always easy to celebrate a friend's success, especially when that friend is a Controller, but if you want to reach out to a Controlling friend, you will need to enjoy their latest accomplishments. You will need to enter their world and celebrate it.

Controllers often operate as rugged individualists because the people around them are either intimidated by their aggressive demeanor or turned off by their self-promoting style. But Controllers still need affirmation.

It doesn't take much to show a Controller you care. They don't need long and deep pep talks. All that is required is a brief affirmation like "Good luck on your job interview" or "I love the colors you chose for your living room." For Controllers it is the affirmation of the moment that counts most.

Controllers may look like they don't need encouragement, but small acts of affirmation are the building blocks to befriending a Controller.

How to Befriend a Withholder

Reaching out to a Withholder begins by building trust. Loyalty is at the heart and soul of any good friendship, especially with Withholders. You need to earn a Withholder's trust by keeping his confidences. Take extra care to protect their privacy—by not probing too deeply and by not disclosing to others the personal information the two of you discuss.

Once a foundation of trust is established, one of the greatest gifts you can give a Withholder is laughter. A good laugh multiplies joys and divides grief. It disintegrates pressure accrued from the daily grind. Humor makes things seem less complicated and less austere. It gives new perspective on serious issues.

In befriending a Withholder lighten up. Act silly. Be spontaneous and playful. Appreciate the delightful sense of the absurd.

CONCLUSION

Instead of having a word for *friend*, Native Americans called a friend "one who carries my sorrows on his back." If you find yourself in a friendship with a Pleaser, Controller, or Withholder, you can expect to feel the weight of their burdens, and you will need to shoulder most of the responsibility for making the relationship work. And you can expect difficulties. Some people will transcend their dysfunctional behavior patterns, but entrenched Pleasers, Controllers, and Withholders will test the patience of even the most sincere friend.

13

Making Love Last a Lifetime

We have an idea that the best marriages begin in a romantic tidal wave that sweeps us off our feet. I have seen first-year college students drop out of school to get married when they scarcely had the first month's rent. Their education was incomplete. Their career plans were not in place. They were far from mature. These freshman-year marriages are sometimes conceived on the idea that she will work while he finishes college and then he will work while she finishes. And they think they will live happily ever after. But of course it seldom works out like that.

Romantic literature and Hollywood have perpetuated the myth that a happy marriage is built on romantic feelings. In the minds of most people, romantic love and marriage "go together like a horse and carriage"—even when marriage flies in the face of good judgment and common sense.

When the inevitable disappointments come and

the infatuation dissolves, the couple gets depressed and thinks they have fallen out of love. But marital fulfillment does not depend on keeping "that loving feeling" alive. It depends on a covenant of the will—a covenant to nurture a relationship that in turn strengthens the individual. Making love last a lifetime depends on the promise two people make to slay love's silent killer: guilt.

HOW GUILT CUTS THE HEART OUT OF MARRIAGE

In a survey assessing "who makes you feel most guilty," the majority of respondents confessed they were the key perpetrators of their own guilt. But next on the list was "my spouse." Thirty-seven percent of married people reported that their spouses control them through guilt.

In this section we consider the four "marriage styles" that result from different mixtures of love and guilt in the same person. We will look at marriage through the eyes of the (1) Pleaser, (2) Controller, (3) Withholder, and (4) Lover.

The Pleaser as a Marriage Partner

The Pleaser—high guilt, high love—lives for affection. They measure and weigh every expression of tenderness like a soldier hoarding water in a desert. The Pleaser's goal in marriage is to maintain emotional intimacy. They thrive on closeness, deep sharing, open communication, and unconditional support.

But the Pleaser's idea of affection is actually a distortion of true intimacy. "If I have to tell my mate what I need or want," they say, "then our relationship is lacking intimacy. And if I have to ask for what I want or need it spoils it for me. I would rather do without than ask." The Pleaser wants a spouse who can provide exactly what they want on demand like a mind reader.

The Pleaser believes any apparent lack of "intimacy" is a serious crack in the wall that sustains the marriage. In order to protect intimacy, they increase their efforts to please.

The husband of a Pleaser, separated from his wife, told me she never stopped cleaning up after him. She showered him with praise. But the symbol of her overeagerness to please was what he called "the pre-smeared toothpaste act." Each morning after brushing her own teeth, she would put toothpaste on his toothbrush as a little message of affection waiting for him when he woke up. "I wish she would stop being so thoughtful!" he told me in exasperation. He became so disgusted by the loving dabs of toothpaste, he began washing them off and replacing them with his own. "And of course, she never stopped being hurt by my failure to reciprocate her kindness," he told me.

To protect intimacy, the Pleaser avoids conflict at all costs. They hide their disappointments and rarely show signs of unhappiness, even when they are fatigued and miserable. They take the smallest portions, the more uncomfortable chairs, and the biggest responsibility. The Pleaser always yields to their partner. They give more than they receive in marriage because they never make their own needs fully known.

The Pleaser is a great pretender. But their role as a "protector" is equally stellar. For example, a Pleaser husband may secretly borrow money to avoid a financial emergency. He won't tell his wife. "Why should she lose any sleep over it?" he reasons. Wanting his wife to be happy, he says things are fine, when in fact they are not. He believes the truth would be too much for his wife to handle. His lying bothers him by adding to his already heavy burden of guilt. But he feels it is worth lying if his wife can be spared anxiety and disappointment.

Kahlil Gibran said, "Let there be spaces in your togetherness." This admonition is hard for Pleasers to follow. Pleasers sometimes unwittingly push away their spouse by trying to hold on too tightly. Since no marriage can thrive on a diet of intimacy alone, the Pleaser's unending efforts to be intimate satiate the spouse and his or her appetite for intimacy diminishes. In fact, spouses who value intimacy most in a marriage are destined to smother their partners, who are equally hungry for space.

The Controller as a Marriage Partner

The majority of Pleasers are women. The majority of Controllers are men. Opposites attract, for attraction is often an attempt to fill the gaps in our own personality. Naturally, then, these two personality styles are attracted to each other, resulting in many Controller/Pleaser marriages.

Conalee Levine-Shneidman, in her book *Too Smart for Her Own Good? The Impact of Success on the Intimate Lives of Women*, writes, "According to the lessons of our childhoods, [the man to marry] was

ambitious, hardworking, strong willed, and successful."
That's a pretty good description of the Controlling
husband. Levine-Shneidman goes on to say that "to
the extent that a woman could find such a man, she
was considered a success herself. To the extent that she
didn't, she wasn't."

The Controller—low guilt, low love—does not
need affection in the same way a Pleaser does. He is
too analytical to focus on feelings. The Controller is
task oriented, a good problem solver. Maybe too good.
He has little patience for sifting through emotional
dialogue. Instead, he wants to cut through the fog
bank of feelings, sort the facts, analyze the problem,
solve it, and move on.

In a matter of moments, the Controller can lay out
a step-by-step plan of action for his spouse to follow in
solving a problem. But his quick-fire solutions do not
make his wife feel understood. His premature problem-
solving increases her needs, which are unmet and
deep-seated. He has taken control of the situation
without showing sensitivity to her need for intimacy.

Controllers have no problem getting their needs met
in a marriage. They take the biggest portions and the
most comfortable chair, and they do not take responsibility for their spouse's feelings. The wife of a Controller
confided in me, "Every day before I go to work, I set up
the coffee machine, and all my husband has to do is stag-
ger into the kitchen and press the button. We had an
agreement that I would make his coffee every day, and
he would bring me flowers once a week. He brought the
flowers for two weeks, and I haven't seen any since. The
funny thing is he doesn't feel a twinge of guilt!"

Unlike the Pleaser, the Controller is better able to

repress guilt and shame, partly because he is able to exploit the guilt feelings of his spouse. More than eight in ten wives say they feel guilty more often than their husbands do, and four in ten say their husbands never feel guilty. Part of the reason is that when things go wrong, women tend to blame themselves, while men blame anything else they can find. A husband's manipulative maneuvers, however, deny both partners the joyful intimacy of marriage.

The Withholder as a Marriage Partner

Withholders, high on guilt and low on love, do not trust their marriage partner. They fear abandonment. And they guard against their anxiety by keeping much of their own life shrouded in secrecy.

Withholders give up on having their needs met by another person. They withdraw into an isolated world of their own where no one is close enough to hurt or disappoint them.

Adult children of divorce are particularly prone to this relational pattern. In a landmark ten-year study on adults who had survived a divorce as children, Judith Wallerstein found that women often select the "wrong" marriage partner because they are afraid to select the right one. "They're so scared of abandonment or betrayal that they pick men they're sure of not losing or don't care about losing," she says. "These women are afraid to risk, and you can't trust or love without risking."

Sons of divorced parents must also protect themselves from becoming Withholders in marriage. Many of them bury the painful feelings resulting from the divorce and become emotionally constricted. As a result, even when they marry they are slow to express their feelings, and they fear rejection and pain.

Withholders can break down their barriers once they realize their anxiety has less to do with the present than with the past. Children who grow up in a family in which the mother or father is not there, or in a home which is emotionally unpredictable and inconsistent, often fear abandonment. As married adults, this fear has little to do with their present spouse and almost everything to do with the home they grew up in.

Withholders sabotage their own efforts at intimacy by blaming themselves for perceived rejection. Since they are watching and expecting signs that say they are not truly loved, they often find them. Because no mate can be consistently caring, the Withholder has ample examples of "rejection." And each time they think themselves rejected, Withholders see themselves as failures. Once again, guilt has sabotaged a loving relationship.

The Lover as a Marriage Partner

Lovers—low guilt, high love—have the capacity to empathize. They analyze their spouse's situation and sympathize with their feelings. They do not expect their spouse to read their mind. And they do not assume blindly that they know what it "means" when their spouse says or does something.

The Lover respects the uniqueness of his or her mate. I have always been annoyed by the traditional candle ceremony in the wedding service. In this ceremony, the bride and groom each take a burning candle and light another candle, then blow out their own candles, symbolizing that the two have become one.

But marriage doesn't work like that. We don't blow out anybody's personality when we get married. Even after years of marriage, partners remain uniquely themselves. Lovers respect this individuality. They know that a healthy marriage is built on a relationship of mutual respect and autonomy. They help the other person develop his or her full potential.

Lovers communicate their needs openly and honestly. What they say is in sync with how they feel and what they want. When they are asked how they feel, they respond with the truth. They do not mask their real feelings to protect their pride or even to avoid hurting their spouse's feelings. Instead, they share their innermost thoughts—the good and the bad.

In my study of the love/guilt styles of more than 1000 individuals, I found many married couples who were Lovers. Marriage seems to help people improve their ability to love. Couples told me that marriage helped them smooth out their rough edges. One husband described how he and his wife changed across the years. "I've become less self-centered," he said, "less goal-oriented and less obsessed with things. She has become more confident and more relaxed."

DEALING WITH A DIFFICULT MARRIAGE

In a *Los Angeles Times* poll, more than 2000 adults said that their main goal in life was to be happily married. We long for the love found in marriage, and more than ninety percent of us find it—at least for a while.

Eventually, however, even the happiest of couples

encounters rough waters. And being married to a Pleaser, Controller, or Withholder only compounds the challenges. Here are some tips for making love last in a sometimes turbulent marriage.

How to Love the Pleaser

Pleasers measure their marital satisfaction by how good they feel. As long as their emotions are riding high, their marriage is a success. When feelings of sadness seep into the relationship, as they always do, Pleasers become anxious and begin to doubt their marriage. For this reason, you need to underscore your commitment to your Pleaser spouse again and again.

Without the trust, security, and assurance that commitment generates, marriage to a Pleaser is bound for trouble. Say to your spouse, "I will be there for you in all the unpredictable days ahead. When everything seems uncertain, you can count on my love."

To love Pleasers effectively, you must also shower them with affection. Pleasers are carrying an excessive burden of irrational guilt, and you can help them relieve some of it by expressing your appreciation for who they are (and not just for what they do for you). A tender kiss, an unexpected and romantic card, or holding hands says to the Pleaser, "You are loved and appreciated for being you."

How to Love the Controller

The key to loving a Controlling spouse is to help him put himself in your shoes. You will need to teach him how to love with his heart as well as his head.

Make it easy for the Controlling spouse to empathize with you by telling him exactly what you want and need. If you need intimacy more than problem solving, tell your spouse flat out. Say, "I had a terrible day at work, and before you try to give me solutions, I'd love for you to just listen to my feelings." At first you may not see any change in your spouse's behavior, but if you consistently let your needs be known, eventually the Controlling spouse will catch on.

How to Love the Withholder

The most important thing a spouse of a Withholder can do is to keep the Withholder from staying stuck. In subtle ways, you may be achieving your identity from enabling your Withholder spouse to need you. Ask yourself if you are doing anything that might subtly make it difficult for your spouse to transcend her self-defeating patterns.

It is also important to allow your Withholding spouse to meet her own needs. You may believe that you are being loving by meeting your spouse's needs, but in truth the most loving thing may be to let the Withholder stand on her own two feet. So pull back. Allow your spouse to take care of herself, and don't always pamper her.

To love a Withholder effectively, you must also be vulnerable. You must allow your spouse to see your joys, fears, values, and life goals. You must take off the mask of calm composure and allow your real self to be known. Your vulnerability will, paradoxically, provide security for your spouse. And the more secure your spouse feels, the more likely she is to make herself vulnerable to you, and thereby transcend her withholding patterns.

CONCLUSION

Long-term fulfillment in marriage does not depend on keeping a loving feeling. It depends on a covenant of the will, a covenant to nurture the relationship. A study of 6000 marriages concluded that nothing is more important in a successful marriage than a determination to make it continue—even if you are married to a Pleaser, Controller, or Withholder. Making love last a lifetime depends on the promise two people make to slay love's unseen enemy: guilt.

14

Raising Healthy Kids

As a parent, which trait would you prefer your child to develop: tolerance for others or obedience to authority? If you are like most parents today, you probably chose tolerance. However, if you were a parent sixty years ago, you would likely have chosen obedience.

The traits parents want to see in their children have changed dramatically during this century. In the 1920s, the top three qualities emphasized by parents were loyalty to the church, strict obedience, and good manners. In a more recent survey, the most valued traits by parents were independence, tolerance, and social mindedness.

There is also a different attitude toward being a parent today. Before the First World War, parents were much more confident. They knew who they were and did not hesitate to impose their ideas on their children. Parents today, broadly speaking, are more hesitant and insecure about their authority role.

However, a child's most fundamental need remains constant—the need for unconditional, constant love. In this chapter we will look at how guilt undermines that love, and how to overcome parental guilt so as to become a more loving and effective parent.

HOW GUILT CUTS THE HEART OUT OF PARENTING

"Is it remotely possible that any other parents in any other age have had the opportunity to feel as guilty in as many ways as we have?" asks Glen Collins in *How to Be a Guilty Parent.* "Did they have PG movies? Dinky Donuts Breakfast Cereal? Video games at the checkout counter?"

Parental guilt stems from two sources: (1) failing to meet unreasonable expectations, and (2) feeling parents alone are responsible for the behavior of their children. Regardless of its source, however, when guilt shows up in a parent-child relationship, it undermines authentic love.

When parents do not recognize and resolve their feelings of guilt, they will project their guilt onto their children, punishing their children for what are in fact the parent's sins. The child then gets a distorted self-image. However, when parents feel good about themselves, are loving and kind, provide a safe home environment, and encourage the child's growth, they offer positive reflections of a child's worth.

Guilt cuts the heart out of effective parenting because it prevents a parent from empathizing with a child. Consider the four "parenting styles" that result from different combinations of love and guilt. Consider parenting through the eyes of the (1) Pleaser, (2) Controller, (3) Withholder, and (4) Lover.

The Pleasing Parent

"From the time a child first asserts his own will," write Dave and Jan Stoop in *A Parent's Cry for Help*, "we struggle with the possibility of our destroying his happiness." This struggle is natural and normal. But for the Pleasing parent, the child's happiness has become an obsession.

Pleaser parents, high on guilt and high on love, usually are prey to the "superdad/supermom" syndrome. They have brought into their parenting unattainable standards, and they punish themselves for failing to reach them. "My guilt is a day-in, day-out nagging in the back of my head," a parent told me. "I feel guilty for not doing everything I know I should do as a parent."

Pleasing parents are permissive and indulgent. They place few demands or controls on their child. And the child never learns to abide by rules and regulations.

Pleasing parents take on unrealistic responsibility for their child's happiness. They turn the pleasures of parenthood into a burdensome duty. Pleasing parents do not go for ice cream or play a game with their child because it is fun to do. They do nice things for their child simply to neutralize their guilt for not being a better parent and to earn their child's love. "I found myself coming back from business trips loaded with more and more presents for my son," a father told me.

Pleasing parents, in a relentless effort to make their

child happy, struggle with disciplining their child and hate to say no. I have heard Pleasing parents confess to feeling guilty for setting a clear bedtime for their children and then feeling more guilt for not sticking to it.

Why do Pleasers have difficulty with discipline? Researchers have found that the more personal guilt a juror in a court case feels, the less likely they are to find a defendant guilty. This same phenomenon holds true for Pleasing parents. Their own self-punishment prevents them from exercising the discipline a child needs to mature.

Unfortunately, when you spoil a child, you are teaching him that he is too weak or incompetent to do things for himself. Spoiled children expect to get what they want when they want it. Without realizing it, by spoiling their child, well-meaning Pleasers are preventing their child from maturing.

The Controlling Parent

Controllers, unlike Pleasers, feel proud of what they do do, rather than feeling guilty for what they don't do. As one father put it, "When I have to work late or travel a lot, I miss the kids. I'm not happy about it, but why should I feel guilty? I'm working for their sake."

Like Pleasers, Controllers may shower their child with gifts, but it is not to calm their guilt. It is to give them more control over their child. Each gift has a string attached: a string for binding the child more closely to the parents.

Controlling parents—low on guilt and low on love—do not suffer from feeling overly responsible for their child's happiness. They are not asking, "What am I doing wrong?" Controlling parents are more preoccupied with producing the perfect child.

Controllers view their children as a sculptor views a mass of unformed clay. They see children as raw material to be formed and molded. Controllers have an end product in mind and work hard to create it. Their dictatorial and unsympathetic style does not give leeway to the preferences and personality of the child. This controlling drive is especially alive in parents who are determined (1) to raise an outstanding athlete, (2) an academically brilliant student, or (3) another professional who follows in their steps in medicine or law.

The Controlling parent sees children as accessories to make the parents look good. So their children learn to conform to their parents' desires. But in the process, these children never develop a healthy identity. Instead, they sacrifice their own wishes and dreams to win parental approval. The end result is emptiness and depression in a grown-up body.

A physician who always wanted to be a missionary came to see me. He told me that being a missionary was not good enough for his father. "I would have been letting him down," he said. "Dad spent a lot of money on my education, and he wants a return on his investment." This accomplished doctor, at the height of his career, was in deep depression, grieving the loss of a dream his controlling father had overruled. "I am sure Dad thought he was being a loving father, but he never considered my desires," he told me.

Controllers anxiously promote the success of their children. They rationalize their desire for vicarious accomplishment and convince themselves that their overzealous promotion is motivated by love.

The Withholding Parent

Withholding parents—high guilt, low love—show their worst side in family relationships. They may be passively withdrawn at work or with friends, but their overdose of guilt often gets the best of them as parents. While their style is sometimes "hands off," providing neither discipline nor loving attention, their parenting technique can sometimes turn ugly, especially when they project their self-punishment on a little person who is at their mercy and can't hurt them back.

Withholding parents often believe children are thoroughly selfish and require harsh discipline. Like the Puritans, they have no qualms about beating the devil out of a child. They enforce strict rules to tame a child's wicked ways. They reason that breaking a child's will is crucial to good upbringing.

Children, however, cannot grow to be healthy adults in the absence of love. For example, during World War II, orphaned babies were placed in new institutions outfitted with fine furniture and brightly colored toys. Care was taken to prepare tasty and nutritious food. Nevertheless, the health of the children began to deteriorate rapidly soon after they arrived at the institution. The children stopped eating and playing. They grew weak and began to die.

United Nations doctors were flown in to investigate. They identified the fatal lethargy as marasmus and described it as "a mysterious and gradual emaciation of the body which seems to strike when others don't take time to show enough love." The doctors prescribed ten minutes each hour for all children to be picked up, hugged, kissed, and talked to. Within a short time, the strange epidemic disappeared. The little ones brightened. Their appetites returned. And they played with their toys once more.

While Withholding parents do not typically inflict blatant neglect on their children, their dysfunctional family lifestyle and legalistic belief system create a home that is as cold and unnurturing as any asylum. Often, these parents are suffering from personal pain that keeps them from giving love to their children.

An adage among the mountain people of East Tennessee says: "Give a dog a bad name and he'll kill himself livin' up to it." Withholders who never learn to balance their discipline with love raise children who eventually turn on them.

The Loving Parent

The loving parent—low guilt, high love—balances law with love and rules with relationship. They balance the best qualities of the Pleaser and the Controller.

Like the Pleaser, Lovers may at times overdo in trying to make their child happy. They may sacrifice sleep, cancel nights out, spend generously on the child, and even become oversensitive to their child's needs. But Lovers give to their child out of love, not out of guilt. Their gift-giving is done with the health of the child in mind.

Like the Controller, Lovers take command, teaching and training a child in the way he or she should go.

They set limits and practice discipline. But Lovers know this control is not meant to last. Tempting as it is to hold on to their power, they know they must relinquish their self-serving dreams as the child matures and goes her own way.

Unlike the Withholder, Lovers tap into their own pain so as to understand their child and comfort her. James Dobson, in *Dare to Discipline*, says that the most successful parents are those who have the skill to get behind the eyes of the child and feel what he feels.

Empathy unlocks the power of parental love. Without it, parents cannot understand the heights and depths of their child's emotional experiences. But with empathy parents can avoid the mistake of projecting their own feelings, needs, and desires onto the child. Empathy allows parents to discover their child's uniqueness. With empathic love, a parent builds a solid foundation of self-worth and dignity that will support a child through the rest of her days. Dr. Archibald Hart says, "When a child is deeply loved at home he can cope with teasing, being rejected by others, failure to meet performance demands, being poor, or lacking physical attractiveness." The parents' empathic love provides a sense of emotional security that is deep and sure.

BECOMING A LOVING PARENT

If you have recognized yourself as a Pleasing, Controlling, or Withholding parent, you will want to reread the relevant section in Part Two for general tips on how to become a more balanced, loving person.

Meanwhile, here are some hints to help you improve your parenting style and become a loving, authentic parent.

If You Are a Pleasing Parent . . .

Let me say this straight out. You will never be the perfect parent. Give up your unattainable standards of parenting and quit punishing yourself for failing to reach them.

If you are a Pleaser parent you want your children to like you—to the point that you have difficulty with discipline. Your biggest challenge as a parent is to establish firm rules and stick to them. Set limits with specific consequences that take place when those limits are tested. Make your rules explicit. Talk to your children about them and be sure they understand what happens when the rules are broken.

As your children grow into their teen years and beyond, you need to guard against jumping to conclusions about what they might need or want. Pleaser parents are often so eager to help their children that they assume they know what their children are needing before accurately assessing their children's needs. To prevent yourself from jumping to conclusions about what they might need, say to your older children, "If I were in your shoes, I would feel . . . But what are you feeling?"

If You Are a Controlling Parent . . .

The greatest disadvantage to being a Controlling parent is your relentless grip on an idealized image of what your children are to think, feel, and do.

Learn to let go. You must relinquish your ideals of the perfect child. That child does not exist. Your son or daughter will do things, many things, that disappoint you. They will have feelings and thoughts that are not what you desire. But for your sake and theirs, allow them to be human. Give them permission to be unique.

Talking without listening is a common fault of controlling parents. A mother wrote to me after reading my book, *Helping the Struggling Adolescent*. She told me that for the first time she was focusing on understanding her two teenage children and learning to draw them out. "I had been so concerned that they hear me that I had neglected to listen to them," she told me.

Bite your tongue and listen to your children. Don't try to mold them into an unnatural form. Instead, discover who your children are. Listen to their feelings without judgment. Say, "Tell me more about it." Express affection for who they are—not only for what they do. Bolster their self-image with verbal and nonverbal expressions that tell them they are loved no matter what. A brief affirmation ("You are a great son") or a gentle squeeze on the shoulder will speak volumes to your children.

If You Are a Withholding Parent . . .

The finest gift you can give your children is a healthier you. If you are high on guilt and low on love, I urge you to consult a counselor and begin charting your course to recovery.

You are most likely suffering from the residue of a

difficult past, and you will unknowingly pass on some of the harmful effects of your background if you do not get help. Getting help for you is one of the most important investments you can make for the health and nurturing of your children.

DEALING WITH A DIFFICULT PARENT

Pastor Charles Swindoll says every family with children is a cross between Grand Central Station and the Indianapolis 500. Comedian Martin Mull says, "Having children is like having a bowling alley installed in your head." Parenting, no matter how you look at it, is tough work.

But learning how to be a healthy child as an adult can be difficult too. Maybe you have learned the art of loving, authentic parenting but are yourself still the child of a Pleasing, Controlling, or Withholding parent. If so, here are some tips for dealing with your own parents.

If Your Parent Is a Pleaser . . .

The tie that binds can also strangle. Children of Pleaser parents often feel smothered by their parents' attempts to relate. Therefore, one of your primary tasks as the child of a Pleaser is to build sturdy boundaries—personal property lines that mark those things for which you are responsible. Good boundaries sustain good parent-child relationships.

Pleasers' boundaries are weak and thin. Only a mere membrane separates them from others. For example, they absorb their children's emotions until they can't tell the difference between what they feel and what their children feel. Their identity is enmeshed with their children's identity.

Without clear boundaries, you are bound to be frustrated with your Pleaser parent repeatedly. So draw the line. Say no when you need to. Set up explicit boundaries that provide both of you with a sense of your separateness. If your mother often drops in without notice, for example, and it bothers you, let her know. Say, "Mom, I'd love to sit and chat every time you stop in, but I just can't do it. It would really help me if we could plan on a specific time so I could focus better when you are here."

Having clear boundaries with a Pleaser parent is essential to achieving a healthy, balanced relationship.

If Your Parent Is a Controller . . .

The most common complaints of children with controlling parents is that the parents do not spend enough time with them and that they rarely express affection. Children typically react to these frustrations either by suppressing their feelings or reacting with anger.

If your parent is a Controller, try to identify the underlying hurt you feel and express it instead of sitting on your feelings or blowing up in anger. For example, if you are hurt because your mother or father does not affirm you, use an "I" message to express your pain. For example, you may say, "I know you're very busy, but you have never said congratulations on my new job, and that makes me feel bad."

If you come to your parents with anger and accuse them of hurting you, they will very likely rationalize away your pain. But if you state how you are feeling using "I" messages, you are more likely to open the way to productive dialogue and bring about healthy changes in your relationship.

If Your Parent Is a Withholder . . .

Because you have been the innocent recipient of your parent's pain, you are a survivor. Knowingly or not, you have undoubtedly been affected by your parent's past and have absorbed the jolts of his or her tough times.

If you want to improve your relationship with a Withholding parent, one of the best paths is through either individual or family therapy. Therapy is not a painless process, but if you are willing to make the investment, it can improve the quality of your relationship.

CONCLUSION

Guilt among parents runs deep. So many strands of hope and fear, of ardent wishes and anxious apprehensions, are tangled together in the ties that bind parents and children. But to maintain a healthy connection, the strand of guilt must be kept from strangling parental love.

15

It's Not Just a Job, It's a Relationship

Ｍore time and energy is spent in work than any other waking activity. Sixty-eight percent of us spend more than nine hours each day on the job, including getting to and from work. And more than one in five of all employed adults bring work home at least twice a week.

Work is consuming. We complain about work. We try to avoid it. We call in sick to get out of it. But however much we may complain about our work, we need it not only for the money, but also for a sense of personal worth. Through work, we find our place in the world, giving of our time and talents to support ourselves and to help others. Freud said that to live well we must learn to love well and to work well. Kahlil Gibran said, "Work is love made visible." Guilt, however, has a way of stealing into all of our relationships—including work relationships—and undermining our productivity and the sense of worth and meaning we derive from our work.

HOW GUILT CUTS THE HEART OUT OF FULFILLING WORK

The number-one cause of guilt in the workplace, for both women and men, for both executives and entry-level workers, is the guilt that results from neglecting the family. The second cause of guilt is failure to maintain control of one's work. Regardless of where guilt feelings come from, few workers would disagree that guilt clogs up the gears of the daily grind.

Let's look at work and guilt through the eyes of the Pleaser, Controller, Withholder, and Lover.

The Pleaser at Work

Pleasers—high guilt, high love—are the kinds of workers every employer covets. They are conscientious and hardworking. Their goal is to make the boss happy. And they do until they overextend themselves by taking on too much.

Pleasers have a difficult time saying no. Consequently, they take on more than they should. They agree to assignments before weighing their ability to follow through on them effectively. Eventually, their eagerness to please results in inevitable failure. Then, of course, guilt skyrockets.

The Pleaser's guilt is deeply ingrained because their self-worth is based on performance. They equate what they do with who they are, and workaholism is the inevitable result, for they cannot take time off without feeling more guilty. They mistakenly assume that the harder they work the quieter their nagging conscience will become, but in actuality they are merely digging themselves into a deeper pit of guilt.

A pastor came to see me because he had become overinvested in his work. "How can I take time away?" he complained. "I haven't had a vacation in years, but I just don't see how I can afford the time off." This well-liked pastor was literally killing himself in an effort to please everyone.

The Controller at Work

Controllers—low guilt, low love—have a high need for achievement. Like Donald Trump, Lee Iacocca, Ross Perot, and many others, they know what they want, and they pursue it with dogged determination.

Controllers' professional lives are built on a false sense of omniscience and omnipotence. Their attempts to control lead to overorganizing and oversupervising themselves and everyone who works with them. As Controllers move up the ladder of success, their unquestioned authority and sense of control leaves their colleagues feeling used.

Controllers tend to base their self-worth on the size of their bonus. They suffer from the I-am-what-I-earn myth. They are not necessarily greedy. They just want a financial base that keeps them in control.

Controllers, like Pleasers, are victims of workaholism. They work unrelentingly and measure success by their productivity. However, the Controller is motivated from within, while the Pleaser is motivated from without. Controllers are "driven" by their unconscious need for personal security.

The Withholder at Work

Withholders—high guilt, low love—live in fear of losing their jobs. They feel undeserving, insecure, and threatened. Their feelings of guilt cloud their efforts to lend a coworker a helping hand. Quiet and reserved, Withholders rarely sense a coworker's feelings or recognize their employer's needs.

From time to time, the Withholder's guilt spills over onto colleagues in the form of a subtle jab or a harsh criticism. But more often they express their displeasure through passive-aggressive acts.

Because Withholders are sometimes seen by customers as aloof and unhelpful, they often function best in jobs that call for high task achievement and low team involvement. They do not have the flexibility or the sense of humor necessary for the give-and-take of organizational politics. They are most comfortable surrounded by piles of work behind closed doors.

The Lover at Work

A man walking along the road came across three workmen employed at a quarry. He asked each worker what he was doing. The first man growled, "I'm breaking rocks." The second man said, "I'm earning a living." The third man replied with a smile, "I'm building a cathedral."

Lovers—low guilt, high love—do not work from a compulsive need to overcome guilt. Their self-worth does not depend on the size of their paycheck or their place in the organizational chart. Lovers work from the sense of fulfillment that comes from contributing and achieving.

The mark of the Lover at work is, of course, empathy. Lovers learn to put themselves in their coworkers' shoes. A few years ago, the Ford Motor Company worked empathy into their company philosophy. They put the saying "Do not judge your brother until you have walked at least one mile in his moccasins" on lapel pins, key chains, and posters. The plan worked. From management to laborers, workers began to treat each other with greater respect.

DEALING WITH DIFFICULT COWORKERS

When asked "What upsets you most about where you work?" employees complained most about their fellow workers. Penn State psychologist David Day has found that job satisfaction depends more on work relationships than salary. How we fit in with coworkers is often more important than how much we make. It is all the more important, then, that we learn how to deal with difficult coworkers and bosses. Here are some tips for getting along with Pleasing, Controlling, or Withholding colleagues.

How to Work with a Pleaser

If you want to improve your relationship with Pleaser coworkers, let them know how valuable they are to the team. Recognize their contribution, not in a patronizing manner, but because you really value what they do.

All too often, Pleasers are taken for granted in the

workplace. They volunteer for tasks that others shun, and they work hard for sometimes little reward. So take note of their contributions and let them know you appreciate their work.

How to Work with the Controller

If you work for a mildly Controlling person, focus on the satisfaction of being needed. He may not express his appreciation for your work, but he does need you. Try showing your appreciation for his work, and he may eventually reciprocate.

An extreme Controller will use compliments, guilt, threats, intimidation, and power mongering to control his employees, and sometimes he will create so much conflict within an organization that working conditions become intolerable. If you work for such a person, set clear boundaries by, for example, writing follow-up memos to clarify your specific assignments and to document the work you have done. If this person's Controlling tendencies continue to interfere with your work and cause you undue stress, seek help through regular company channels or even through professional counseling. Ultimately, however, if the Controller is making your life miserable and no change is in sight, you may need to leave your job.

How to Work with the Withholder

The famous orchestra conductor Leonard Bernstein was once asked to name the most difficult instrument to play. He replied, "Second fiddle."

Although it is often tough to let others get the

praise for a job well done, the most gracious gesture you can extend to a Withholder coworker is to help him or her look good. Work enthusiastically without recognition to help your Withholding colleague accomplish an important task. As a result of your loving attention, the Withholder may develop trust, confidence, and the ability to work well with other people.

CONCLUSION

Whether you are working with a Pleaser, Controller, or Withholder, it is difficult to go wrong in the workplace if you are making yourself indispensable to the people around you.

Dr. Hans Selye, the acknowledged "father of stress," studied the effects of stress in the workplace and observed that stress is reduced when we make a constant effort to win the gratitude of our fellow workers. Selye rephrased the biblical admonition "Love thy neighbor as thyself" into his own personal code, "Earn thy neighbor's love." Rather than trying to accumulate more money or power, he suggested we acquire goodwill by helping our colleagues. "Hoard goodwill," Dr. Selye advised, "and your house will be a storehouse of happiness."

16

Relating to God

We were designed with an emptiness, a gaping need. In *The City of God*, Augustine expressed this universal human feeling when he said, "O Lord, thou hast made us for thyself, and we are restless until we find our rest in thee." Without an authentic relationship with God, we are left anchorless and detached.

A relationship with God has many of the same qualities of any other relationship. But it is different. For one thing, anyone who wants a relationship with God must accept the fact that God is a Spirit. And, as Jesus told the woman at the well, "His worshipers must worship in spirit and truth" (John 4:24). Some people might find it easier to relate to a god of gold or one that lives in a mountain spewing fire and steam. We can't, however, have a loving relationship with a gold statue or a fiery mountain.

So how does a mere mortal develop a relationship with God, who is Spirit? In this chapter we explore the most important relationship of our lives—our relationship with God.

HOW GUILT CUTS THE HEART OUT OF RELATING TO GOD

Martin Luther once said, "Most Christians have enough religion to feel guilty about their sins, but not enough to enjoy life in the Spirit." I know people who are deeply serious about religion, but they are so obsessed with their sins that their religion actually does them more harm than good. These people equate feeling guilty with being spiritual and, in their heart of hearts, do not want forgiveness. They would rather grovel in their self-generated guilt.

Thankfully, God does not call us to a life of self-abasement. He, in fact, wants to release us from condemnation. As Jesus said, "Come to me, all you who are weary and burdened, and I will give you rest. Take my yoke upon you and learn from me, for I am gentle and humble in heart, and you will find rest for your souls. For my yoke is easy and my burden is light" (Matt. 11:28–30).

Consider the kinds of relationships with God that develop in the lives of the Pleaser, Controller, Withholder, and Lover.

The Pleaser and God

Pleasers—high guilt, high love—have a faith that feeds primarily on emotion. They pride themselves on being "holy fools," simple, unsophisticated Christians who serve God spontaneously and enthusiastically.

They care more about "experiencing" God than they do about theology, and they are often anti-intellectual. But the problem with this "holy fool" mentality is its lack of intellectual integrity. A faith that is not supported by reason is shaky and susceptible to the siren call of cults and TV evangelism hucksters.

A relationship with God based on emotion is prone to periods of self-defeat, worthlessness, and self-condemnation. Pleasers generally "know" God loves them, but they often feel they aren't doing enough to please him. In an effort to deserve God's love, they are forever striving for perfection. When they fail to meet their self-imposed standards, as they always do, God becomes a much feared prosecutor, judge, and jury. Pleasers then placate their overly sensitized conscience by endless service and self-sacrifice. Pretty soon they find themselves caught up in a vicious cycle of feeling guilty, confessing, feeling relieved, and then falling back into the same behaviors or attitudes that caused the guilty feelings all over again.

Because fervent feelings, even among the most devout, eventually burn low, Pleasers will often suffer from burnout. A sustained emotional high puts a strain on the human system and leads to psychological problems. People who are given to easy ecstasy, for example, are the ones who are most vulnerable to serious depression.

The Controller and God

Controllers—low guilt, low love—relate to God on a cerebral level. They weigh the evidence for accepting or rejecting religious beliefs and have a faith that is based primarily on analytical reasoning. Their analytical emphasis has dried up any fervent affection. As Isaiah put it: "These people come near to me with their mouth and honor me with their lips, but their hearts are far from me" (Isa. 29:13).

Unlike Pleasers, Controllers place great value on facts. They are not motivated to give money or volunteer by emotional, guilt-laden appeals about hungry children or battered wives, since they know it is impossible to meet every need in the world. They want adequate information before they volunteer their time or money, and they will only give when they have analyzed the situation and believe in what they are being asked to do.

Controllers often take God for granted. God, for the extreme Controller, becomes a good old boy, a pushover, someone to help him out in a jam. The Controller may rationally understand what a relationship with God is and may affirm such a relationship. However, mental affirmation alone is not what a relationship with God is all about. It takes experience of God for a meaningful relationship to develop.

The Withholder and God

The Withholder—high guilt, low love—has a wobbly faith that teeters on the precipice of doubt. Withholders doubt themselves. And they doubt God.

Because Withholders had parents who were harsh, strict, and demanding, because the love they received from their parents was conditional, Withholders see God as someone to avoid and placate. They view God as vindictive, stern, angry, controlling, and impersonal.

Withholders have often encountered cruel life experiences. They feel abandoned by God, and they feel devastated and angry. Withholders' prayers are often reduced to a single word: "Why?" They ask it again and again, and God seems impervious to their query.

The Withholder's relationship with God, however, is not hopeless. Through time, doubt can lead to faith.

The Lover and God

Lovers—low guilt, high love—have a faith that balances their heads and hearts. They use their reason to distinguish what is true from what is false. To increase their understanding of God, they read their Bible, they learn about theology, they attend Sunday school classes and Bible studies. They are alert to false teachings, and they use their knowledge of Scripture to test what they are taught.

Lovers, however, do not stop with merely an intellectual understanding of God. They also seek experiences of God. They enjoy praise and worship, and they look for answers to their prayers. Knowing their own limits, they give of their time and money to help others.

Jonathan Edwards, the preacher who began the Great Awakening of the 1740s in New England, knew the importance of balancing reason and emotion. When another pastor, Charles Chauncy, criticized the emotional excesses of Edwards's audience, who often screamed, shrieked, and fainted, Edwards replied, "I should think myself in the way of my duty, to raise the affections of my hearers as high as I possibly can, provided they are affected with nothing but truth."

Lovers achieve a delicate balance between heart and head because they are not weighed down by guilt. They accept that they cannot change the past, but they work to alter the way in which their past affects their present condition. As Paul declared, "Therefore, if anyone is in Christ, he is a new creature; the old has gone, the new has come!" (2 Cor. 5:17).

Lovers accept God's forgiveness, and they believe his promise: "I have swept away your offenses like a cloud, your sins like the morning mist. Return to me, for I have redeemed you" (Isa. 44:22). With joy, they realize that "there is now no condemnation for those who are in Christ Jesus" (Rom. 8:1).

BECOMING AUTHENTIC LOVERS

God knows we are not saints. We all struggle with Pleasing, Controlling, and Withholding patterns, both in our relationship with him and in our relationships with friends, family, and coworkers. But he came to set us free from these unhealthy patterns of relating, to show us how to love—authentically, joyfully, freely.

The following three people are examples of people whose lives changed as a result of their relationship with Jesus Christ, the source of love. They were not good Lovers to begin with. They struggled with shame, guilt, self-condemnation, and self-centeredness. But because they believed in Jesus' power to heal and to save, they could not help but change. Through their relationships with Jesus, they transcended their guilt and became authentic Lovers.

Barbara: How a Pleaser Became an Authentic Lover

Everyone at church liked Barbara. She was the first to arrive on Sundays and the last to leave. She taught Sunday school and helped out in the kitchen at the church's weekly suppers. She volunteered for endless projects, and when missionaries came, she turned her purse inside out to help support them.

But in her effort to please everyone, Barbara was failing the people who mattered most to her—the members of her own family. After eleven years of marriage, Barbara's husband left her to raise three kids on her own. The emotional jolt, however, did not slow Barbara down. If anything, she had a tougher time saying no.

One Wednesday evening at church, an associate pastor confronted Barbara with her frenetic pace and her compulsion to please. The next morning Barbara called my office. We met later that week and began uncovering the reasons behind her compulsive need to please. We worked at setting boundaries, relaxing, and focusing on the important rather than the urgent. We explored the family she grew up in, her broken marriage, and her feeling responsible for everyone's wellbeing. One session seemed to be the turning point for Barbara.

"I was reading about Mary and Martha this week during my devotions," she told me. "I've read the account a hundred times, but this time I realized that I have been so consumed with *doing* good things that I have been missing out on *being* with Jesus."

Barbara still struggles with being too busy. She has

to work hard at saying no to insure quality time with her children. But Barbara has moved from an addiction for pleasing to a healthy self-concern for personal development. Two years ago she earned a master's degree in English and became a teacher in a local community college.

Wayne: How a Controller Became an Authentic Lover

Wayne was a success. In his early forties, he was a vice president of an international corporation. He was married, and his daughter was doing well in college. Wayne was on his church board, and his pastor consulted him regularly.

Then Wayne attended a large Christian men's conference in another state. He listened to well-known speakers and enjoyed the inspirational singers. On the second night of the conference, he met with a small group for a time of discussion and prayer. Each man talked openly about his personal struggles.

When it was Wayne's turn to speak, he unexpectedly broke down. "I'm selfish, I'm so selfish," he cried. Tears began to flow as he told stories of manipulating his wife, daughter, and coworkers.

During that pivotal moment in the hotel room Wayne renewed his relationship with God and committed himself to love more authentically. He still has difficulty showing his emotions, but he works at being vulnerable and empathetic. As a result, his relationships have improved, and he is enjoying new intimacy with his wife and camaraderie with his colleagues.

Maggie: How a Withholder Became an Authentic Lover

Maggie carried more undeserved guilt than anyone I know. Having suffered serious neglect as a child, Maggie struggled with a painful psychosomatic illness. A faithful church attender, Maggie always sat toward the back of the sanctuary on an outer aisle seat. She avoided eye contact and would speak softly when spoken to.

Most people avoided Maggie because talking with her was awkward. But not Leanne, our pastor's wife. She often greeted Maggie before and after each church service.

At lunch one day with Pastor Jack and Leanne, I observed, "Maggie seems to be changing."

"What do you mean?" Leanne asked.

"She smiles and seems warmer. She is wearing brighter colors, and last Sunday she initiated a conversation with me."

Leanne's face lit up. "Isn't it wonderful?" she said. "A few months ago, I persuaded Maggie to join a Bible study group that meets here in our home. At first she didn't say much, but we kept encouraging her to speak up, to tell us what she thought. Pretty soon she came to the Bible studies smiling and eager to share what she was learning!"

Maggie is still shy and sometimes awkward in conversation. She will never be the life of the party. But in a simple Bible study with caring people, Maggie encountered Jesus and broke out of the shell that kept her in isolation.

THE GREATEST SOURCE OF LOVE

The journey toward authentic love is difficult. Often our patterns of Pleasing, Controlling, or Withholding are so deeply engrained, so unconscious, that we despair of ever being able to change them. But as these stories and countless others show, the Holy Spirit is at work in our deepest, most hidden places, using Scripture, circumstances, books, and other people to expose our self-defeating behaviors and encourage us to overcome them.

Yes, the journey is long. You will spend your whole life learning to love. But if you believe in Jesus Christ, you already have the greatest source of love dwelling within you and causing you to grow. For, as John, the beloved disciple of Jesus, wrote: "If anyone acknowledges that Jesus is the Son of God, God lives in him and he in God. And so we know and rely on the love God has for us. God is love. Whoever lives in love, lives in God, and God lives in him. In this way, love is made complete among us so that we will have confidence on the day of judgment" (1 John 4:15–17).

Complete love. Confidence on the day of judgment. A life without the fear of condemnation or punishment. We have all this and more through Jesus Christ. What more could we possibly ask for?

Notes

Chapter 4: What's Shame Got to Do with It?

1. W. Hugh Missildine, *Your Inner Child of the Past* (New York: Simon and Schuster, 1971).
2. *Philadelphia Inquirer*, August 13, 1984.
3. Anne Morrow Lindbergh, *Gift from the Sea* (New York: Pantheon, 1975).
4. Martin E. P. Seligman, *Helplessness: On Depression, Development, and Death* (San Francisco: Freeman, 1975). See also S. F. Maier and Martin E. P. Seligman, "Learned Helplessness: Theory and Evidence," *Journal of Experimental Psychology: General* 105 (1976), 3–46.
5. Viktor E. Frankl, *Man's Search for Meaning* (Boston: Beacon Press, 1962), 75.

Chapter 5: Godly Sorrow

1. Dr. Bruce Narramore, *No Condemnation* (Grand Rapids: Zondervan, 1984).

Chapter 7: Identifying Your Relational Style: A Self-Test

1. The "Trait Test" is reprinted from J. E. Crandall, "A Scale for Social Interest," *Journal of Individual Psychology* 31 (1975): 187–95.

Chapter 8: Compulsive Love: The Pleaser

1. Anthony de Melo, S. J., *The Song Bird* (Chicago: Loyola University Press, 1983), 138.
2. Carmen Berry, *The Messiah Trap* (San Francisco: Harper & Row, 1988).
3. Bernie Siegel, *Love, Medicine, and Miracles* (San Francisco: Harper & Row, 1986), 172.

Chapter 9: Covenient Love: The Controller

1. Morton Kelsey, *Caring: How Can We Love One Another?* (Mahwah, New Jersey: Paulist Press, 1981), 188.
2. John Powell, *Why Am I Afraid to Love?* (Tabor, 1967), 111.

Chapter 10: Reluctant Love: The Withholder

1. M. Scott Peck, *The Different Drum* (New York: Simon and Schuster, 1987), 227.
2. Ibid.

Chapter 11: Authentic Love: The Lover

1. Daniel Batson, K. O'Quinn, J. Fultz, M. Vanderplas, and A. M. Isen, "Influence of self-reported distress and empathy on egoistic versus altruistic motivation to help," *Journal of Personality and Social Psychology* 45 (1983): 706–18.
2. Henri Nouwen, *The Wounded Healer* (New York: Doubleday, 1972), 38.
3. M. Scott Peck, *The Road Less Traveled* (New York: Simon and Schuster, 1978), 83.
4. Lewis Smedes, *Mere Morality* (Grand Rapids: Eerdmans, 1983), 50.

Chapter 12: That's What Friends Are For

1. Alan Loy McGinnis, *The Friendship Factor* (Minneapolis: Augsburg, 1979).

DR. LES PARROTT III is a professor of psychology and director of the Center for Relationship Development at Seattle Pacific University. He holds an M.A. in theology and a Ph.D. in clinical psychology from Fuller Theological Seminary. The author of *Helping the Struggling Adolescent* and *A Counseling Guide*, Parrott has also written articles for *Christianity Today*, *Moody*, and *Focus on the Family*.

▓ HarperPaperbacks *By Mail*

GET THE LIFE YOU WANT WITH
THREE MIRACULOUS GUIDES FROM
NEW YORK TIMES BESTSELLING AUTHOR
DR. WAYNE W. DYER

YOUR ERRONEOUS ZONES

The #1 bestseller with over six million copies sold. Learn to break free from the trap of negative thinking that can act as a barrier to your success and happiness, and take control of your life. From self-image problems to over-dependence upon others, Dyer gives you the tools you need to enjoy life to the fullest.

PULLING YOUR OWN STRINGS

Dyer reveals how to stop being victimized and operate from a position of power in this multimillion-copy, #1 bestseller. A modern-day classic, this remarkable guide offers dynamic techniques for coping with the frustrating situations of everyday life that stand in the way of your happiness and personal destiny.

NO MORE HOLIDAY BLUES

For many of us the arrival of the holiday season brings disappointment, stress, and loneliness. But Dyer shows us how we can recapture the true spirit of the season with wise, easy-to-follow advice for making the season — and the rest of the year — bright.

**For Fastest Service —
Visa & MasterCard Holders Call
1-800-331-3761**

MAIL TO: Harper Collins Publishers
P. O. Box 588 Dunmore, PA 18512-0588
OR CALL: (800) 331-3761 (Visa/MasterCard)

Yes, please send me the books I have checked:

☐ YOUR ERRONEOUS ZONES (ISBN: 0-06-109148-0) $5.99
☐ PULLING YOUR OWN STRINGS (ISBN: 0-06-109224-X) $5.99
☐ NO MORE HOLIDAY BLUES (ISBN: 0-06-109147-2) $5.50

SUBTOTAL...$_____
POSTAGE AND HANDLING...................................$ 2.00*
SALES TAX (Add applicable sales tax) ....$_____
TOTAL:...$_____

*(ORDER 4 OR MORE TITLES AND POSTAGE & HANDLING IS FREE! Orders of less than 4 books, please include $2.00 p/h. Remit in US funds, do not send cash.)

Name _____

Address _____

City _____

State _____ Zip _____

(Valid only in US & Canada)

Allow up to 6 weeks delivery.
Prices subject to change.

HO 691